"By taking a fresh approach to the subject of project management, sets out in brilliant fashion three elemental principles that make done on time and under budget."

**Grant P. Lungren**
**CEO, Grantlun Corporation**
**Construction Management Solutions Provider**

"Don't begin a project without first reading *Finish What You Start*. An inexperienced project manager will perform with the confidence of a professional and an experienced project manager will find tips to become better."

**R. Schorr Berman**
**Founder, MDTA LLC**

"*Finish What You Start* is a must-read for anyone involved in managing people or process. It provides the essential tools and frameworks we all need to compete in an increasingly complex, time-driven global marketplace. The book's crisp style, no-nonsense advice, and comprehensive roadmap to project management techniques make it a necessary part of every manager's and leader's library."

**Thomas M. Koulopoulos**
**President, Delphi Group**
**Author, *Smartsourcing***

MICHAEL J. CUNNINGHAM

# finish
## what you
# start

### TEN SUREFIRE WAYS TO
### DELIVER YOUR PROJECTS ON
### TIME AND ON BUDGET

KAPLAN ❭ PUBLISHING

This publication is designed to provide accurate and authoritative information in regard to the subject matter covered. It is sold with the understanding that the publisher is not engaged in rendering legal, accounting, or other professional service. If legal advice or other expert assistance is required, the services of a competent professional should be sought.

President, Kaplan Publishing: Roy Lipner
Vice President and Publisher: Maureen McMahon
Senior Acquisitions Editor: Michael Cunningham
Development Editor: Trey Thoelcke
Production Editor: Caitlin Ostrow
Interior Design: Lucy Jenkins
Cover Design: Jody Billert, Design Literate
Typesetter: Maria Warren

Published by Kaplan Publishing,
a division of Kaplan, Inc.

Printed in the United States of America

06  07  08  10 9 8 7 6 5 4 3 2 1

**Library of Congress Cataloging-in-Publication Data**

Cunningham, Michael J.
    Finish what you start : 10 surefire ways to deliver your projects on time and on budget / Michael J. Cunningham.
              p. cm.
    Includes index.
    ISBN-13: 978-1-4195-2366-3
    ISBN-10: 1-4195-2366-X
    1. Project management.  I. Title.
    HD69.P75C86 2006
    658.4'04–dc22
                                                    2006003120

# DEDICATED TO

*The higher Power that controls all of our projects.*

# 1

# INTRODUCTION

*"I am not sure I should have dared to start; but I am sure that I should not have dared to stop."*
**Winston Churchill**

**S**elf-help books and seminars have moved from a specialty to a mainstream genre in recent years. We can learn from Anthony Robbins how to focus and get more from our lives, look to the influence of spiritual leaders to increase internal well-being, or discover leadership lessons from Rudy Giuliani.

Looking to improve our lives, we search for insights and strategies that will help us make a difference; frameworks, lessons learned, and directions that will lead us to improved paths for personal and professional success. Surprisingly enough, while there is much to find on topics such as management and personal development, there is little that deals with our first major challenge in our adult world: How do I manage a project?

Project management is something that most of us learn by experience. That is the hard way. Becoming an effective project manager is something almost everyone wants, yet our first project management experiences are often embarrassing failures. Relevant training in the principles or best practices associated with projects and processes seem to be missing from schools and colleges everywhere. Most of us become effective project managers through our "project experiences," building on the good, the bad, and sometimes the ugly outcomes.

## EVERYONE IS A PROJECT MANAGER

Whether we are repairing a car, remodeling a kitchen, or coordinating a family event, project management skills are important to us. Being able to control the resources, time frames, and variables to deliver a satisfactory result has a tremendous impact on our lives. It dramatically influences how others perceive us—affecting careers, relationships, partnerships, and our ultimate success.

While we may not have the title in our job descriptions, almost every individual relies on being able to manage a project to some degree or at least must be able to identify and hire someone who is good at project management.

Most of us have envied the people who just seem to be natural born project managers. Organized and tidy; calm when things are moving off schedule; able to facilitate and convince others to agree to changes that need to be made. All their projects seem to transpire successfully. Do you ever feel that you will never be able to emulate them? Do you really want to receive that same level of praise and achievement?

That is the purpose of this book. Nobody is born with project management skills, or leadership skills for that matter. They are learned, observed, practiced, and refined.

*The goal of this book:*
*To make even the most inexperienced individual*
*into an effective project manager,*
*and make good project managers*
*even better communicators.*

This increase in your project management skills will provide a framework for important changes in your life, whether making career moves, lifestyle modifications, or tackling individual projects.

## A NEW AND SIMPLER APPROACH—THE KEY TO SUCCESS

Project management is often viewed as a complex topic, made more so by gobbledygook terminology and how project information is communicated. (Anyone here know what a Gantt chart is?) Acronyms abound, and special graphical renditions and difficult-to-use software all create resistance and barriers for budding project managers. It doesn't have to be this way.

*Finish What You Start* provides a simplified and transparent road map that anyone can understand and use to manage projects without all the aforementioned baggage. Simplicity is important because *everyone* needs to understand the steps and actions in your project plan. This immediately improves your effectiveness as a project manager regardless of the size of the project.

This book will help novices and experienced professionals alike understand that project management is not just about documenting and measuring what needs to be done, but about proactively managing a series of processes utilizing simple-to-use tools, frameworks, and positive communication techniques. We will examine the principles of the most successful project managers, what makes them tick and how they get things done right and on time.

Fundamental to your success with this book is adopting an approach to project management based on documenting and simplifying processes. Every project is a series of processes, and once this is understood, everyone can begin the journey of improving his or her project management skills.

Three fundamental building blocks support this simplified approach; first *Plan,* then *Implement,* and finally *Manage* the project. Each of these is outlined in detail with easy-to-follow examples, terminology, and skill-building exercises.

The bottom line is that anyone can benefit significantly from this simplified approach.

## WHAT'S IN IT FOR ME?

If you want to reduce risks, improve potential outcomes, enhance teamwork, and deal with project problems before they become serious, then this book can help you. *Finish What You Start* provides the framework to get things done on time and on budget.

Even the most seasoned project manager looks for improved means to reduce costs, improve time lines, and reduce risk from projects. This simplified approach makes all project activities transparent to those involved with the project. As a result, goals, objectives, tasks, and responsibilities are clear to all concerned.

Whether you are interested in learning the fundamentals of managing projects or are looking to fine-tune the skills you have acquired over time, *Finish What You Start* will help you become a more effective, successful project manager.

# 2

# SKILLS TO BUILD ON

**W**e all possess some skills and characteristics that will help us become more effective project managers. It does seem, however, that some are just natural-born "project guys." You know whom I mean; their desks were very clean in grade school, homework tidy and on time, seemingly perfectly organized all the time. Does that make them great project managers? Perhaps not; however, they did display one of the most important skills: *organization*

The good news for the mix of skills and methods needed for successful project management is that we all have some of them. Each skill has three characteristics: the skills themselves, our competency level, and our personal experience level exercising them.

We begin by outlining skills important to becoming an effective project manager and what we can do to start using and improving them.

# PERSONAL CHARACTERISTICS

## Organized, Neat, and Tidy?

Turns out our personal characteristics are an important starting point for improving project management skills. Starting with organizational skills, individuals who are effective at laying out a beginning, middle, and end to a project plan already have a significant advantage. Their organizational skills reflect the mind-set required for the first phase of any project: *the planning phase.*

A tendency for people with excellent organizational skills is then to move on to important issues, such as making sure they have the tools and materials to do the work. They also consider useful questions such as:

- Do I have access to the research required for the project?
- Do I need assistance to complete the work?
- Are resources to do the job available?

The bottom line is that powerful organizational skills provide a significant advantage in early project management experiences. Fortunately, those not blessed with these skills at birth can learn them. Throughout this book are references to areas where an organizational framework will help build your skills and improve work patterns.

*"Don't agonize. Organize."*

Florynce Kennedy, civil rights activist

Another aspect of organizational skills is the tidiness factor. There is no question those who automatically put things in places where they can readily find them make their life easier. Individuals who keep the most important information relevant to the project readily available and maintain organized desktop and computer files have an unfair advantage in project management. Thank your lucky stars if you are born with the organizational and tidiness traits or have learned them early in life.

Here is not the place to get into physiological or psychological reasons why some are "more organized" while others have a more random pattern to their life. As far as this book is concerned, both groups can benefit from project and organization frameworks. There is help on hand for those of us who are untidy. Although a Feng Shui world would be a wonderful vision, the chaos, confusion, and challenges that beset a project in progress mean we have to learn to deal with changing elements as best we can. (After all, even Feng Shui projects started out untidy!)

Even if you find your persona rebelling against a seemingly huge challenge of changing organizational skills and behavior, consider the benefits of project management frameworks and collaboration tools for all projects. These may assist your career and personal life in ways you do not yet recognize.

How much translates from the management of your projects to the rest of your life varies from individual to individual. Our goal is not to create a place for everything and everything to be in its place, but rather to control the various elements of projects that are important. We want to teach you ten surefire ways of getting the work done and getting it done with a repeatable set of tools. These will increase your chance of successful outcomes.

## Confidence (Not a Skill but a State of Mind)

*Regardless of where you are . . .*
*skills you already have can leverage*
*your personal characteristics, giving the*
*confidence to create great outcomes*
*for all your projects.*

How do you rate yourself? Are you a superconfident individual? Perhaps you are a little reserved or even a wallflower? Regardless of where you are on this continuum, current skills can leverage personal characteristics, giving you the confidence to create great outcomes for all your projects. Confidence increases for a number of reasons. You know you can produce the advertised results—you have done it before; you have the experience, or as a London cab driver might say, "We have the knowledge."

In some cases, we have confidence because we don't know what we cannot achieve. This can be especially important in the teen years and early 20s. Many take on projects that seem impossible today, but in retrospect we look back at mountains successfully climbed. This builds confidence. Regardless of the size of the project being planned, being comfortable with your own capabilities and the skills of others in the project has a direct influence on results. This is particularly important for projects that are more difficult or break new ground. Having attained the goal once before and assembling a team with the desire to succeed and prior experience will reduce risk dramatically.

You see where I am headed. Part of the confidence that you have in yourself is directly related to the selection of those on your team and their potential; their previous results; their ability to work with you. This confidence can cause working relationships to last a lifetime. Whether a fan or not, Clint

Eastwood makes no bones about his project activities when producing and directing films. He works with people he knows he can rely on, even personal friends. He understands that things do not always go perfectly in any project, and making movies may be one of the biggest project management challenges; where art meets science in a very special way.

One risk reduction strategy from Mr. Eastwood's perspective is to use the same team. This creates fewer surprises and provides greater consistency from one project to the next. He has confidence in his team, and his ability to get the project done on time and on budget increase.

## COMMUNICATION SKILLS

### Does Everyone Understand What's Going On?

Communication skills are one of the most important elements in any project—or in life for that matter. One individual is a highly successful communicator creating more valuable project outcomes versus others who are not. Therefore, determining how to communicate with individuals on your team and taking an inventory of personal communication skills is critical. Consistent, high quality communications to our team will make a huge difference.

It is worthwhile reviewing how others view you personally from a communication perspective. Do they see you as the strong, silent type? When you participate in a conversation, do the people sit and listen or do people ignore you? When communicating about projects, it is important that people understand with clarity what it is you are saying; and of course why you're saying it.

The following quotation from Plato makes the point in an amusing way:

*"But can you persuade us, if we refuse to listen to you?" he said. "Certainly not," replied Glaucon. "Then we are not going to listen; of that you can be assured."*

Plato

Now this might sound simple, but it is probably one of the most important aspects of effective project management; ensuring that others truly listen to your communication has a huge impact on whether they understand it. Even more important is what action they're likely to take as a result.

Each individual has different communication strengths and weaknesses. Project management deals with many different mechanisms to communicate what is happening at a given time. So considering communication strategies for effective project management, we have to either build on our own strengths or overcome weaknesses in this area.

In general, less is more when it comes to communications. Winston Churchill once wrote a famous letter to Dwight Eisenhower that took several pages. Churchill apologized to Eisenhower that he didn't have time to write a shorter letter. As an outstanding communicator, Churchill makes a very valid point. Taking the time to provide the information needed in the most succinct and economical manner will increase the chance of the reader's understanding and perhaps even gaining agreement with your point of view or statements.

*"Listening, not imitation, may be the sincerest form of flattery."*

Dr. Joyce Brothers

## Increasing Your Communication Effectiveness

One of the challenges in communicating information about projects and project status is determining what information is relevant for the particular group you're dealing with. The easiest way to understand this and take the appropriate action is to do the following:

1. Identify the audience.
2. Craft the message.
3. Determine the action to take as a result.
4. Use the most effective means to deliver the message and then overcommunicate.

Using these steps can avoid a lot of misinformation in general project management. Taking these four steps ensures that the information is accurate and that the recipients are clear on the appropriate action to take. In a simple example, assume you are doing a remodeling project in the kitchen. You have to talk to the contractor about some things that are not working out, either on time or on budget. Responding by sending a flaming e-mail—assuming that the contractor even has e-mail—would be the wrong approach to deal with this issue. The contractor may or may not realize there is a problem, but by setting the tone in such a harsh manner, you run the risk that the contractor may reject all or some very relevant concerns. You've heard the old adage, "You can catch more flies with honey than with vinegar." People do not normally respond well to being accosted.

A better approach is to document the originally agreed expectations on timing and budget and then ask for the contractor's recommendations to bring things back in line. This nonaggressive communication should be your first line of action.

Applying the four-step approach to this situation can alleviate the problem peaceably and improve your communication characteristics at the same time.

Crafting the message is another important element that affects the individual's understanding of a project; ensuring it is accurate can avoid serious miscommunication. Otherwise, others' perception may be the exact opposite of your own. This matters whether you are the project manager or a contributor on the team, as many situations arise because of misunderstandings caused by a poorly communicated message. Crafting a clear message—even if you are just picking up the phone and providing status on something—it is still important. When reporting the status of a project to your supervisor, it may also be necessary to include what action is needed to avoid delays if the project is in danger or running over the budget. Is a review meeting with your supervisor and/or your team necessary? As we build on later in the book, managing a project successfully requires a high level of communication skills and discipline.

Determining what action you want people to take as a result of communication is also vital. An inference in the wrong direction will cause others to be defensive and create a detrimental response to either you or the project.

There is no need to take a position of neutrality, but think through the *cause and effect* of your communication. Consider what you want others to do, what actions they should take, and the advice you want them to follow. Try putting yourself in their position, if possible, and if you are sending it via e-mail please *read it carefully* before pressing the send button. There's been many an e-mail sent where the unavailable "retrieve button" was required. This is because senders did not consider the full impact of their communication before issuing it. Some of these e-mails become famous as they reach the public. In 2005, the Mike Brown messages from his stint at FEMA emerged after his resignation following Hurricane Katrina and clearly illustrated a need for some improved communication skills. There is no question he would have used the "retrieve and destroy" function if it ever existed.

The last step in communication is the method. In any team everyone has different communication preferences. Some find their personal cell phone the least attractive means of communication and favor e-mail. For formal communications about the project, particularly where action is required, the need exists for some form of paper or electronic trail. This can be useful if something is not initially recognized and is inadvertently neglected or deleted—you can resend it or bring it to the sender's attention. In today's environment, with many decisions made via a combination of electronic applications and verbal discussions, keeping track of activities and discussions is essential. So many staff- and Internet-enabled PDAs make it simple to ensure information reaches its target.

A final request is to ensure you overcommunicate. Some might say overcommunication can be as big a problem as not communicating enough. My experience is that this is not the case and that many of us, particularly beginners at project management, tend to undercommunicate. A simple status message released on a regular basis helps, even one just highlighting areas of change. Send status messages to affirm that the project is on time and on budget. Doing so creates confidence in your team as it is informed, building credibility for yourself as a project manager. It is clear that you are in control of what's happening with the project and that you care enough as the project manager to inform members of the team that things are going well, not just alarming them because things are going badly.

Each of us has our own communication style, and my goal here is not to smother that character but rather to bolster its likely success within the framework of a project. Although these four steps relate to communication within projects, using them should prove useful in almost any aspect of your professional or personal life.

In addition to following these steps and guidelines, it is also worthwhile to invest in improving your communication skills.

*"When people express themselves verbally,*
*they want feedback that they've been heard,*
*and they also want to be understood. This is true*
*even when they don't understand themselves,*
*as is the case when an upset person tries to*
*describe their feelings and thoughts.*
*But when two or more people want to be heard*
*and understood at the same time, and no one*
*is willing to listen and understand, an argument*
*or exit is almost inevitable. For this reason, a*
*masterful communicator makes it his or her goal*
*to listen and understand first, before attempting*
*to be heard or understood."*

Dr. Rick Brinkman and Dr. Rick Kirschner,
*Dealing With People You Can't Stand: How to*
*Bring Out the Best in People at Their Worst*

## Improving Important Communication Skills

Of all communication skills, the written word is one of the most important. In many cases where written instructions are integral to a project, these skills can never be good enough, always leaving room for improvement. There is a reason that many organizations employ communication specialists to document how products are to be assembled, maintained, and operated.

The same applies to processes and procedures that are a key part of almost every project.

Becoming a project manager does not require you to become a professional author, but your written skills need to be proficient. Project members demand that the information you are presenting is concise, clear, and understandable. An investment in improving writing skills has a manifold payoff when it comes to effective project management. As more projects require the use of the Internet, Web conferencing, and remote management, effective communication in written form can make the difference between success and failure.

> *"Conflict occurs when the emphasis in a relationship is on the differences between people . . . You get along better with people when the emphasis is on similarities between you. The difference between a conflict with a friend and conflict with a difficult person is that with a friend the conflict is tempered by the common ground you share. Success in communication depends on finding common ground before attempting to redirect the interaction toward a new outcome."*
>
> Dr. Rick Brinkman and Dr. Rick Kirschner,
> *Dealing With People You Can't Stand: How to Bring Out the Best in People at Their Worst*

My own organization has been involved with many off-shore development projects, and even though off-shoring is now a standard mechanism of doing business for many operations, it has also resulted in many failures. Many of these are associated with cultural and language miscommunications and misunderstandings. Your personal investment in written skills will not go unrewarded. Others involved in your projects will have a much greater understanding of what your intent is, your message will have precision, and you will limit silly but expensive mistakes.

Another area worth investing in is improvement of your verbal communications. During the early stages of my career, in order to move up the chain of command in the organization, I had to face my most feared specter: public speaking. Many today learn to deal with this challenge in school or college, but it still remains a fear for many.

As Dale Carnegie essentially said in his most famous books on public speaking, anyone can become an effective, or even outstanding, public speaker given the desire to do so.

The four steps for communicating described earlier can be a good reference point for public speaking, with one big difference: you are the communication vehicle. Once again:

1. Identify the audience.
2. Craft the message.
3. Determine the action to take as a result.
4. Use the most effective means to deliver the message and then overcommunicate.

There are many reasons why investing time and energy into public speaking is worth it—most important being because it will dramatically improve your project management success rates and effectiveness. In addition, if you learn how to get your point across and persuade people of your point of view, your cause, and your goals, imagine the impact this has on your day-to-day project management results. One excellent example is a man in his 20s I know well who was concerned every time he had to address his class at school, and he carried that concern to university. Determined not to take this problem onward in life and having selected a marketing communications degree in career direction, he understood that he had to deal with the difficulty and soon.

He overcame the problem by becoming part of the freshman orientation program at Boston University. During his first year in that program, he had to greet, meet, organize, and speak to more than 1,000 students during orientation, assisting with large start-up meetings bringing new freshmen through the process that he had been through the previous year. This was not just a programmatic public speaking activity, but it also meant he had to deal with questions and problems in a public forum.

Although initially intimidating, the benefits of this activity became huge. After graduation he entered the workforce as a marketing executive for an international advertising agency. The point: Although we can systematically deal with some communication issues, we have to go for it if we really want to become an outstanding communicator. Make the decision to increase your skill and begin a public speaking program. Increased skills in public speaking and writing will not just help the content and outcomes of your project management activities, but will also help your confidence.

## COLLABORATION SKILLS

During the communication section, we mentioned the importance of creating a friendly but effective environment for the project and that we need collaboration skills to take this to the next level.

When learning how to collaborate effectively, creating and blending into a team is paramount. Even the most senior managers in the country—Bill Gates, Jack Welsh, the president of the United States—all rely on their team and *teamwork* for successful project outcomes.

The emphasis on teamwork is for a good reason. Teamwork is not just the foundation of a successful project; it is the keystone for success. Creating an organization and environment that fosters teamwork is not as difficult as you might think.

Even in organizations that appear to reward individual leaders and not their teams, the project manager who understands that the team is the engine will be the long-term winner. Getting the team working together as a cohesive unit is the difference between success and failure.

> *"Dependent people need others to get what they want. Independent people can get what they want through their own efforts. Interdependent people combine their own efforts with the efforts of others to achieve their greatest success."*
>
> Stephen R. Covey, *The 7 Habits of Highly Effective People*

For the teamwork to be effective, collaboration skills provide a platform to make it happen. Collaboration skills are not just soft skills but also include the expert use of collaboration technologies. Web conferencing, telephone conferencing, secure chat, bulletin boards, and wireless technologies provide an environment that cuts barriers and allows an almost seamless integration of project members.

These technologies and their affordability mean they will be the baseline for many collaborative projects in coming years. It will be important to be proficient in managing collaborative efforts using these systems, and it's not as easy as you might think.

Although technologies to create or join a Web conference have become ubiquitous, how many Web conferences have you attended that were compelling, effective, or even exciting? The difference is not just being able to use the technologies competently but understanding how to collaborate and communicate using them.

We mentioned earlier in this chapter that many individuals have their own preferred means of communication. In project management this can be good and bad. Depending on personal preferences, it may be necessary to modify your medium according to the individuals involved.

For project managers, the only way to resolve this problem is to become competent with all the common tools and collaboration systems out there. Fortunately, many of these are now a standard part of many corporate and governmental environments, so the opportunity to learn how to use them effectively is abundant.

## ATTITUDES

Having the right attitude is the starting block for effective collaboration. For a project manager, respect for team members, understanding their roles and what they contribute, and having empathy are all important.

Respect, understanding, and empathy are characteristics that help any project manager's attitude improve. They also have a direct effect on results. As with any management activity, project management relies on setting and managing attitudes, culture, and expectations competently.

*"There is little difference in people, but that little difference makes a big difference. The little difference is attitude. The big difference is whether it is positive or negative."*

W. Clement Stone

If these are not set or managed well, the effects may be lack of support from team members or a desire from team members to avoid involvement in the project.

In either case, this is not a good situation. The military understands the importance of keeping the team focused, working together, and maintaining the respect of all the members.

Once respect vanishes from a project, members participate primarily out of fear or retribution; the most likely result is project failure. Again, this is the wrong place to start any project or program. Personal attitudes dramatically affect how you manage any project. If you believe in the project and put together a good plan, it is much more likely others will follow, garnering an excitement and desire for tremendous results. Of course, the converse is also true: If you signal you really don't care about the project, that this is a job you didn't want to take on, and that you don't want to be leading this project, then those messages will make it very clear to everyone else on the team that this is not very important to you.

*"If you want to get somewhere you have to know where you want to go and how to get there. Then never, never, never give up."*

Dr. Norman Vincent Peale, *Positive Thinking Every Day: An Inspiration for Each Day of the Year*

Attitude is never more important than when managing tasks or projects that are not our favorites. Being able to handle and manage them as well as projects that we really are excited about often makes the difference between an average and outstanding project manager.

Have you ever noticed how really excellent project managers seem to create excitement even when given projects outside their normal scope of responsibility or even with just plain dull and boring projects? These are the people who are going to garner huge success in their careers going forward. Creating excitement and positive attitudes gets the project team jazzed and contributing. Handling the mundane projects without complaint leads directly to more rewarding ones in the future. Success with simple projects leads to more complex and interesting assignments.

Therefore, attitude is something that is tremendously important and even though it is not a skill, it is something that can be relearned.

*"The greatest discovery of any generation is that man can alter his life by altering his attitude of mind."*

William James

The link between attitude and collaboration within the project cannot be underestimated. Body language and underlying messages do not transmit as easily over the phone, within e-mail messages, or via a project plan as they do in a face-to-face meeting.

The most fundamental of all collaboration skills is the ability to run a meeting. It might sound too simple a place to start, but running a meeting is really the basis of any project management plan.

*Respect, understanding, and empathy*
*are characteristics that help any*
*project manager's attitude improve.*
*They also have a direct effect on results.*

## RUNNING A MEETING

As you will see later in the book, for effective project management, it is required to *plan, implement,* and finally *manage* the project. If we accept that the center of all successful project outcomes is competent oversight, then each project has many management points during its progress. These management points are frequently meetings.

Meetings are control points for the project, where we determine what direction to take and how much progress has been made. So if we cannot run a meeting effectively, we are going to have a lot more difficulty managing something as complex as a project.

Not to overstate the obvious, but running a meeting can be simple with sound planning and execution. All we have to do is plan, lay out an agenda and objectives, and determine who should be there. If preparation is required for the meeting, we need to outline what the session's goals or expected results are. Of course, we have to deal with the logistics, such as checking the attendees' availability and confirming that the needed resources are in place.

Running your first meeting can be almost as daunting an experience as your first public speaking event. Understanding your role and using the appropriate collaboration and communication technologies and skills reduce the risk of failure and dramatically increase the potential of a good result.

TABLE 2.1 *Sample Agenda*

**Starting a Project**

Project:

Date:

Attendees:

Names and company:

| TIME | TOPIC |
| --- | --- |
| 9:00–9:15 | Introduction(s) |
| 9:15–9:45 | Review of project requirements and objectives |
| 9:45–10:15 | Roles, activities, and assignments for the project |
| 10:15–10:30 | Agreement and refinement of project goals and objectives |
| 10:30–10:45 | Wrap-up and next stages |

How many wasted hours in business and other meetings occurred because someone didn't prepare or have the right people there? Perhaps some of the right people were there but not enough to achieve the objectives; no one remembered that some were in different time zones; people integral to the meeting were overlooked; important reading materials were not circulated in advance for participants; or the meeting was not run tightly enough to produce the needed results.

Running a meeting might sound like a simple thing, but running it successfully is more complicated. *Conducting a successful meeting is the most important baseline for your success as a project manager.* Therefore, do not stop at preparing the agenda

Three ingredients important to any successful meeting:
  1. Prepare
  2. Prepare
  3. Prepare

for the session; ensure that everyone who needs to be there is there and that all are armed with the required information for the session.

The simple six-point checklist in Table 2.2 reduces the potential for failure in any meeting. Preparation is a key ingredient to any successful meeting. As you create the agenda, carefully consider the agenda order and the points requiring coverage in order to reach the next review or decision stage. In addition, you should ensure involvement by the right people at the appropriate time and preparation of the needed materials.

Do not assume all those attending will prepare in the same way. If they need to read or review other materials in advance, make sure they understand that will be required. That way, you will not have to waste valuable time updating those who did not prepare effectively.

TABLE 2.2 *Successful Meeting Checklist*

1. Review and deliver agenda.

2. Permit adequate time for review.

3. Ensure allocation of the right time frame.

4. Prepare and deliver relevant documents.

5. Install and review collaborative technology.

6. Send meeting reminders one or two days beforehand.

Estimating how much time to spend on a topic is one of the most difficult aspects of setting an agenda. Remember that attendees often have different perspectives, ideas, and learning curves—some even have their own agenda. There are those who will remain silent till they have something relevant to say, and others who want to say something regardless of its relevance. The longer you have team members present without participating, the greater the likelihood of boring them to death. No one wants to be a meeting wallflower for hours on end. Treat their time respectfully, and good results are more likely to emerge.

There is a formula that has existed over the years illustrating the quality of results from meetings. The *quality of decisions and results* is equal to the *meeting agenda* plus *required attendees* over *time taken to prepare*. The bottom line is preparation and attention to detail pay time and time again.

$$\text{Quality of decisions and results} = \frac{\text{Meeting agenda} + \text{Required attendees}}{\text{Time taken to prepare}}$$

Once the meeting starts and you're running it, team members will expect you to take a leadership position. Just because you are not the most senior person in the room does not mean that you should not take charge. This is a very crucial point. *You must take a leadership position if you are running a meeting.* It doesn't mean you turn into an obnoxious megalomaniac, take the best seat at the head of the table, and start behaving like Genghis Khan. (Believe me, I've seen some people turn into another person given a little seniority.) This is not the way to get your team established and on the right track, but understand that competently running the meeting requires your leadership and guidance.

When in your first project management meetings, it is important to understand the relevance of changing roles. In some situations you will be participating in a meeting or project as a team member with specific responsibilities for components of the program; in other situations, you are the team leader or the project manager. Regardless of your role, you have a responsibility to make the overall project and the team more successful.

Understanding the alternate role of team member and team leader adds greater value to all the projects with which you are involved. At the same time, you must also provide guidance—where you have more experience or knowledge in one area than do other team members—and direction from a management perspective, ensuring that a project does not change its time line or budgetary requirements from goals set at the outset.

Running meetings bring us to another important skill: facilitation.


## FACILITATION

Facilitation is one of the more complex, soft skills essential for project managers. It is not easy to document what makes a good facilitator, as there are many aspects to this skill.

The definition of *facilitate* is "the ability to make something easier to do or understand"; in fact, to simplify. In the context of project management we often see a broader definition. Facilitation is a skill to help us gain agreement. As a facilitator, you'll learn that situations where change is required will face you constantly.

Facilitation skills are composed of a series of competencies; most important are monitoring and understanding what is happening in the project at a given time. This helps you determine if there is a need to facilitate at all. If things are not progressing as planned, or disagreements in goals for key milestones occur, you need to call on your facilitation skills.

Usually, facilitating change in an existing project means a combination of modifications. This might include simplifying a project that has become too complex or changing the resources, time lines, and even deadlines of the project if simplification alone is not the answer.

An effective facilitator possesses:

1. Subject matter skills

2. Expertise

3. Knowledge about the project and the participants

4. Patience and understanding

Therefore, facilitation skills can be learned, but they are also dependent on experience and subject matter expertise. For example, I may want to facilitate a project management meeting about a new building, but I would not be effective at debating with the architect about the structural integrity of the project. Why? Because I do not possess the subject matter expertise. If you do not have the subject knowledge, an expert is needed to help facilitate change, at least to provide relevant input.

I could, however, be a facilitator in a software management project where I do have the subject matter skills, the market knowledge, and the experience. Some facilitating skills relate to earlier discussions on communication and effective collaboration. As a result, it is possible to help facilitate change in direction in a meeting or project by tapping into the experience and subject matter expertise of others on the team.

> *Facilitation Skills Improvement Checklist*
> 1. Identify workshops and learning events to assist development.
> 2. Seek coaching assignments where your skills can be tested and practiced.
> 3. Look for mentors who will help your career and personal development.

Skills development can also improve facilitation skills. Any opportunity that you get to learn how to run workshops can be a great exercise in facilitation skills. Educational workshops or workshops where you are trying to gain agreement are both excellent ways of learning and sharpening facilitation skills. Try to find coaching situations that also help teach facilitation while dealing with changing circumstances. These are beneficial to improving overall project management skills.

In fact, in the world of workshop management programs, coaching is usually the entry-level position. It puts you in the position of providing guidance to some members without having to facilitate and run the workshop until you have the required level of experience.

## TEAMWORK AND TENACITY

Let's return to teamwork, as it is the whiteboard where all the skills come together. Teamwork is often embedded in an organization's culture; in fact, whether a culture of teamwork is present becomes apparent quickly. Regardless of whether

FIGURE 2.1  *Training and Improvement Opportunities*

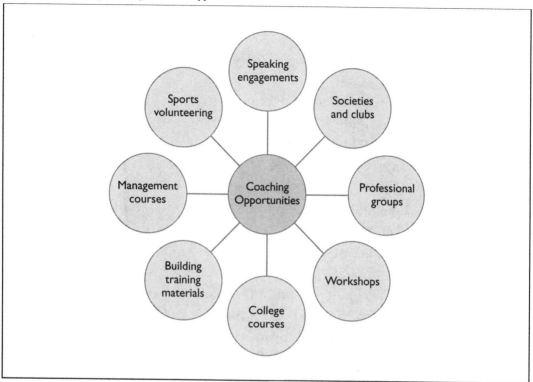

the organization encourages teamwork, make a personal commitment to make it part of any project you are managing within the organization. Create your own personal commitment for your and your team's desire to succeed, not just to bully others into going along for the ride. Strong-arm tactics work only for the short term and often have long-term lingering effects.

> *"A boat doesn't go forward if each one*
> *is rowing their own way."*
>
> Swahili proverb

The last area that fosters teamwork and focuses a team is tenacity. There are many famous quotes about its importance and for one good reason. *Just wanting a desired outcome from a project does not guarantee success.* Project managers have to roll up their sleeves, get others to follow, and keep at it.

*The person who takes no risks guarantees no results.*

Some projects have goals that are a work in progress; they often require huge innovation and risk taking to meet those goals. The first attempts to reach the moon with the Apollo program, the space shuttle, or the design of the airplane were all results of someone's having a vision, a concept of making it happen. Most important, the team was tenacious enough to keep at it until the job was done and the goal was reached. Each failure along the way helped to remove obstacles, eventually resulting in success.

Our skills for project management are in constant development. We learn from one situation and make mistakes, integrate that knowledge, and apply it more effectively the next time. One thing is for sure regardless of your skills, confidence, or experience level: use whatever you have. Get out there and try. The person who takes no risks guarantees no results.

Step up to the plate, get ready to use your skills, and take a swing at it. Oh, and remember to enjoy the game along the way.

# 3

# WHAT'S TO MANAGE?

**B**efore getting into the details of managing the management process for projects, we need to look at what it is we are managing. Rather than giving huge lists of terminology that may put you to sleep, make your eyes glaze over, or cause you to begin a screaming fit, let's take a different, simplified approach to projects. It is not as complex as you might think.

There are only five primary elements in a project. The five things to manage and worry about are

1. *budget*—how much there is to spend;
2. *resources*—the tools and materials required to get the job done;
3. *people*—those who help make it happen;
4. *time*—how long it will take to complete; and
5. *guidelines*—rules and instructions to be followed for the project to have a successful outcome.

While there are many other aspects to project management, all elements of a project fit into these categories. Some might argue that people are resources and vice versa, but I disagree. People are different from materials, tools, and systems, and should be identified and managed as such. It is unusual to hear any project managers trying to persuade a resource such as a pie chart tool to help them, but it is frequent among staff.

Understanding each of these elements makes it easier for you to deal with the next phase of this book as we address the fundamentals of a simple, three-step project management process. The next chapter discusses the relationship between these elements, using a simplified project management approach.

For now, we start by examining and understanding these elements—the parts that comprise a project, that help us clearly understand how to adjust, manage, compensate, and measure throughout the course of the project.

## THE BUDGET

Arguably, the budget should not be the first item. However, in most projects the limits in costs are established before reaching the planning or estimating stage. This makes sense when you think about it; there's no point in looking to build a 3,000-square-foot home if you really only have the budget for a 2,000-square-foot one. If the budget isn't there, then stop before you start.

Another reason for looking at budget first is project success; a project that is hugely over budget will reach a point where it is no longer successful. One example is a home-building project where the $200,000 estimate climbs to $300,000.

Do the homeowners consider that they have received an additional 50 percent in value? Most likely not, and they will consider this a failure unless they carefully reviewed and authorized the changes in advance of any further actions on behalf of the builder or contractor.

If the budget is not reasonable, this is a good point to scrap the project before starting. The opposite of this book's title *Finish What You Start* becomes "Stop Before You Start." If someone asks you to do something that is impossible using your knowledge, resources, and people, and then recommends a figure substantially below what your budget expectations are, then stop; responding will be a waste of time.

> *Nothing is impossible in the world of fiction.*
> *REALITY CHECK: Most projects are nonfiction.*

Developing project proposals for business or personal use and the estimates associated with them are excellent examples of this practice. A contractor offers to help you with the remodeling of your bathroom and estimates $1,000 in labor plus materials. The workers come and overshoot the budget by another $1,000. Whose fault is it: the contractor who didn't make it clear that his workers would spend twice as much time and resources or you as the project manager? The budget and the project were not managed. In this example, the purchaser was at fault. The contractor was working on a time and materials basis, and the purchaser did not monitor what was happening in the deal.

Over my career I have been asked many times to do projects at absurdly low budgets. The only thing I regret is that I didn't tell the people *no way* earlier in the process, without investing time and energy in a detailed proposal they could never afford. Everyone wants something for nothing if they have no budget. That does not help the project manager unless the funding is coming from another source. Determine right at the beginning whether project owners are truly serious in trying to fund this project.

*Everyone wants something for nothing*
*if they have no budget.*

Budgets come in all shapes and forms. In some cases, time or materials are donated to a project. These can have a beneficial impact in some cases or can increase costs.

In bathroom remodeling, someone finds a source for some granite, and you decide to use it because you made a great deal on the granite. It is priced lower than the other manmade-based fixtures being considered, or may even be the same price. When looking at this in detail, some other costs start to emerge; more expensive sinks are needed and they have to be cut into the granite by a specialist. Then the floor needs marble tiles because they complement the granite, increasing costs fivefold from the initially budgeted ceramic tiles.

Despite my earlier negative comments, there is one alternative when the budget seems completely out of whack with what needs to be done: cut the scope of the project before it goes any further. This happens more frequently than you might think, and is often better than the alternative: doing nothing at all on the project.

For example, consider the case of a planned trade show marketing event that has its initial marketing budget reduced. In order to go through with the trade show, resources and costs required adjusting. The following changes ensued:

1. Reduction of booth sizes
2. Decrease in staffing requirements to man the booth
3. Adjustments to travel and accommodations
4. Project plan revision

# RESOURCES

Resources represent the tools, materials, and systems required to get the project done. Our remodeling example may require many resources to complete the job, including tiles, grout, underflooring, screws, and all manner of power tools.

Some resources have a static cost associated with them. A static cost being a one-off cost such as the 30 tiles needed for the project. If the estimate is correct, that is what the project will use. However, some resources have variable costs with them as well. For example, if I don't have the power tools needed for the project; it may be necessary to purchase them. If they are too expensive, it may be more cost effective to rent them—by

TABLE 3.1 *Resources and Their Applicability*

| Materials | Tiles, grout flooring | Paper, binders |
|---|---|---|
| Tools | Drills, sanders | Computers, printers |
| Systems and services | Delivery service | Internet service, software applications |

determining whether the rental period will be enough to get the job done in the time allocated.

Here we see a little wrinkle on the resource variable if we are renting a resource; we have to worry about how long it will be needed and how that translates into budget change. Another factor in our example is whether we need to hire someone to do the job, and, if so, whether he or she already owns the specialized tools required to get the job done. An expert with a nail gun is most likely able to put together a large construction project more rapidly than someone else armed only with the traditional hammer. All of these affect our resources and costs for the project.

So we have tools and materials, but we also have systems. Many of the projects that we are dealing with today have a *system* involved. That system might be a delivery mechanism such as FedEx or DHL or it could be an internal computer system to increase the performance of a sales organization.

A system such as a Customer Relationship Management computer system could meet this need. Once in place, it would track many of the project activities associated with dealing with customers, such as capturing new leads, developing new proposals, and fulfilling prospective customer requests, all within a single system. So the resource that we need to do the job can be a physical resource like a *tool* or *material* or it may be a *system* that we use as the vehicle to help get the job done.

Many resources help us manage projects, such as spreadsheets, visual diagrams illustrating what is supposed to happen in the process, and other project management software used to track these various elements. Resources require us to consider a few different components, particularly as they relate to costs. (See Chapter 4 for more on this.)

# PEOPLE

Of all the things in a project that are a challenge to manage, nothing is more variable than the people. For this reason, I differentiate people from resources. Obviously people's participation means their assistance is essential to the success of the project, but they need managing in a way different from blocks of concrete or computer systems.

Generally, their involvement varies according to

- what they are contributing;
- the type of work being performed;
- their assigned roles in the project; and
- the results required from their participation.

Each of these points is important to capture, as they affect goals and objectives, not just the time or skills added to the project plan. The role of the individual (or collective team) ensures that important assignments are not missed.

The role definition gives us a very specific way of describing people's participation in the project. For example, the manager may be involved with reviewing a document as a project activity, so the role there may be as *reviewer.* Conversely, certain people may be involved with creating some original copy for the document, in which case the role would be document *author.*

It is important that roles are well defined, particularly where many different job responsibilities and characteristics are involved in the project. Take the example of Customer Relationship Management. The roles of people involved in various stages of creating a proposal might range from *sales administrator, customer sales representative, marketing manager,* and *sales support representative.* In certain processes *vice president of sales* or a *contract manager* could be involved depending on the part of the sales process being managed.

If you want that process in your project to be repeatable, and you don't want it to be dependent on whether an individual is in the office at a given time, it is essential that the project be defined using roles. This will allow you, at a later stage, to make specific name assignments while maintaining the same process and assignments.

Another reason using roles is beneficial is that it ensures you are thinking and gaining agreement about who's going to do various elements of the project. As we move to project planning in Chapter 4, the benefits of creating this type of groundwork will become clearer.

TABLE 3.2 *Roles in a Customer Relationship Management Project*

| ROLE | DETAILS |
| --- | --- |
| Inside sales representative | Telephone and Web sales |
| Sales administrator | Administrative support for the sales organization |
| Sales representative | On-site and in-the-field representative |
| Sales engineer | Technical support specialist to support the sales staff |
| Sales manager | Team manager with specific quota and responsibilities |
| Sales director | Manager with greater responsibility |
| Vice president of sales | Head of sales operation |

If your project is small and less complex than just described, you may not need to use role names. For example, if you know the names of the builder, the contractors, and the people inside your organization who are going to do this project, then ensure they are identified in the plan.

# TIME

How many times have I used that phrase in my life? In the case of project management, time is an important factor because it gives us an indicator of two items: First, when the project is supposed to be completed, often dependent on other factors such as budget; and second, the number of resources and people assigned to meet the deadline set.

*There are only two variables in life:*
*time and how we use it.*

We attempted to complete one such project at home several years ago with extremely tight deadlines. This resulted in having to multitask several activities at the same time instead of connecting a series of tasks over a longer time frame.

Because the project was well managed by a general contractor, up to 20 people were working in our yard, all working on different tasks in a cohesive and effective manner. The result was a job done on time and on budget.

*"Time is free, but it's priceless. You can't own it,*
*but you can use it. You can't keep it, but you can spend*
*it. Once you've lost it, you can never get it back."*

Harvey Mackay, syndicated columnist

When we look at time in relation to a project, we consider a couple of things. First, the overall time it takes to complete the project—effectively setting up a deadline for completion—and then the measurement of time from the beginning to that deadline in much smaller chunks.

Breaking the time into these smaller elements is paramount to understanding its impact throughout the project. There are three types of time measurements within the project:

1. Activity or task-based time—how long it takes to complete a particular task

2. Elapsed time—the time between tasks and the next activity

3. Total time—the total project or process completion time

An example of a task-based time measurement activity might be the time taken to lay a new subfloor in a bathroom. This would include time to prepare time for materials in the floor, place cement on the floor, and finally lay the floor material in place.

In the context of the total project for retiling the bathroom, a series of tasks and the time taken are added together to reach the total.

Table 3.3 shows various tasks in this project such as preparing and laying the floor, cutting tiles, laying tiles, preparing the subfloor, and finally laying the tile. Each of these has its own actual completion time. However, simply adding these elements together does not give you a complete, accurate picture

TABLE 3.3 *Time Measurements and Their Purpose*

| TIME MEASUREMENT | EXPLANATION | EXAMPLE |
|---|---|---|
| Task or activity time | Total elapsed time to complete a task | Task time to lay tiles on the floor—3 hours |
| Time between tasks or activities | Time taken between each task that needs to be measured to know the total time for a process or project | Elapsed time between completion of above task/activity and grout drying—5 hours |
| Total completion time | The time to complete an entire process or project, including a total of task time and elapsed time for an entire process or project | Total time to lay the floor including elapsed and actual time totals—8 hours |

of the time it takes to get the job done. This is because it does not show *elapsed time*—the time between tasks. This is the time taken to collect materials and to break for lunch, and all other factors affecting how quickly the project is completed. A major problem when estimating projects is not factoring the impact of elapsed time on outcomes. A major reason why this occurs is that we don't want to pay for elapsed time.

In reality, elapsed time does affect the project and so must factor into the overall deadline. Here is a simple example to illustrate the point: You need a new brochure designed for your department and contact the designer and the copywriter. They provide you with an estimate for a total of eight hours' work—four for the copywriter and four for the designer. Does that mean that your brochure will be finished by the end of the day? Not a chance!

The reason this is unrealistic is obvious: The copywriter and the designer are not the only people involved in the process; someone has to brief the copywriter about what to write,

FIGURE 3.1 *Elapsed Time and Actual Time in a Maintenance Project*

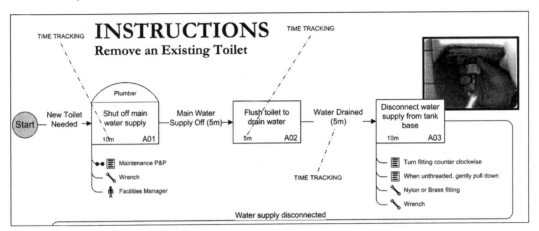

the characteristics of the target audience, and which corporate standards to follow to complete the job successfully. The same is true for the designer; he or she needs to know which standards and characteristics are important for the success of the brochure.

Even if you had an experienced copywriter and internal designer following well-defined standards, it still would be impossible to complete the job in eight hours. That's because others are involved in reviewing, modifying, and approving various iterations of this project.

If you remember these three time principles—activity, elapsed, and total—particularly in project estimating and project management, then time management and measurement errors are less likely to come back and bite you unexpectedly.

Of course, there is another factor associated with time—*time is money*. In project management this adage holds especially true. In order to control the project, you must establish the relationship between time expenses and budget. The cost to meet a deadline can sometimes outweigh the benefits associated with hitting that date, which may or may not be critically important.

*Time is money. In order to control the project,*
*you must establish the relationship*
*between time, expenses, and budget.*

Part of this process is establishing the overall project deadline. The origin of the word *deadline* is interesting. *Dead* and *line* in the same word do not conjure up a pretty picture, particularly if it is missed. Of course some deadlines aren't really deadlines. However, if you miss the deadline to submit your story before the newspaper goes to press or the television station goes on-air live, then it may cost someone a lot of money and maybe even cost you your job. This is a true deadline.

Professionals who are used to working with deadlines have a clear understanding of what makes them important. Newspaper reporters, television journalists, and marketing communication professionals all work to make sure the copy hits the press before the advertising deadline or in time for the 6:00 news.

When we select a fixed date and tie our project to an event or a time line that will not move, we have set a deadline and now have to manage the project from that point. If it looks as if we are going to miss the deadline, then all we can do is change the scope of the project, increase the resources and people involved, or, as a last resort, reduce the quality of the project.

There are a few projects that have a deadline in this form. A good example was the Year 2000 projects in the computer industry. Organizations had to determine whether their applications would catastrophically fail with the new millennium clock change. The result was a massive shift in project activity in the IT sector, the like of which no one had ever seen before or may ever see again.

The deadline was fixed. You either decided to do something, or you held your breath and did nothing. Interestingly enough, a lot of countries outside the Western world did not have the money to address this issue even though some of their critical infrastructure systems needed this attention. As it turned out, Year 2000 IT systems remediation was a bit of a hoax.

Determining a reasonable deadline for the project and then setting the actual date may be a product of high-level strategic goals or forced as part of the business or organizational activity.

*The deadline is an expectation*
*that needs to be managed.*

For example, in a merger or acquisition of new companies, processes and procedures may have to align with the acquiring company over a period. Otherwise, you never gain efficiencies sought as a result of synergies expected from the merger or organizational changes. These usually have some deadline associated with them, and in later chapters we discuss more about setting and managing deadlines. It is safe to say here that the deadline is an expectation that needs managing. If an accurate estimating step has been missed to determine whether you can meet a deadline, you are setting yourself up for failure. If you think you can complete the project on time with resources and staff available, be very sure before committing your own reputation. It may be on the line as a result of your commitment.

# GUIDELINES

The final management variable is *guidelines*. As the word denotes, guidelines are the rules, policies, and procedures required to complete the project successfully and to a satisfactory outcome. Guidelines are different from resources. Resources are the materials, tools, and systems to complete the activity. Guidelines enforce the existing business rules, quality standards, governance, and compliance for successful project completion.

In many cases, we may be relying on the subject matter expert to provide compliance within certain guidelines. For example, we expect that the electricians working in residential or commercial marketplaces are licensed and competent regarding the rules and regulations for that particular country or region. We assume that what they recommend and implement on the job meets the required electrical codes, as we are neither electricians nor familiar with that code. We expect them to ensure that our project follows these important guidelines.

Many aspects of a project have safety, security, or legal implications. Many of these do not rely solely on the knowledge of the subject matter expert to make sure that the job is completed satisfactorily. External or government-licensed inspectors should be checking to make sure that's the case.

Whether we're looking at projects to ensure that financial systems are meeting legal requirements for reporting or that insurers are following regional or country guidelines, some level of guidelines govern each project. As project managers, we need to understand what they are and determine how we meet them.

In other cases, the guidelines provide specific instructions for an activity within a project. Assuming that some field maintenance is occurring in an engineering project, we need to en-

FIGURE 3.2 *Guidelines for Replacing a Toilet*

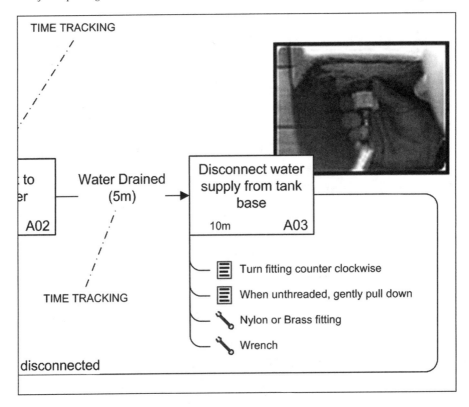

sure that the field maintenance technician has the most up-to-date information. These guidelines could be instructions for a maintenance procedure; they might be an engineering change; or a material safety and data sheet indicating that some procedure has to be followed. This information needs to be included as part of the project plan. If it is, the chances of meeting and following the requirements increase.

As with the discussion in the earlier section, roles and included guidelines often directly relate to the expertise, knowledge, and experience of those doing the job. For example, if you are removing and reinstalling a toilet in your home, chances are you will need some specific instructions on how

FIGURE 3.3 *Toilet Replacement Project with Details*

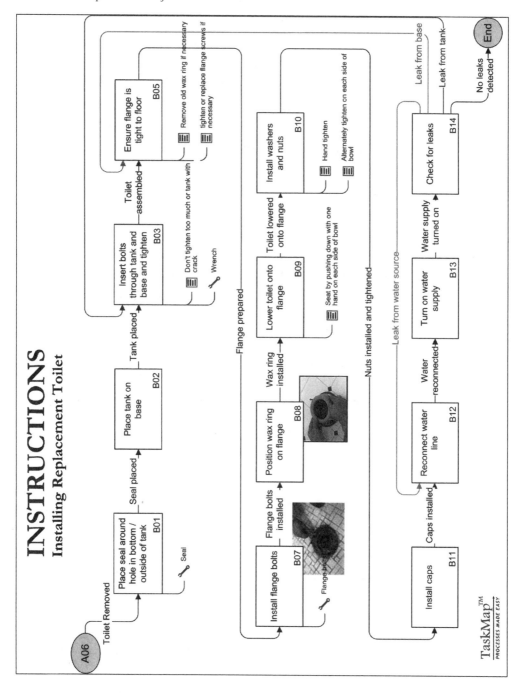

## INSTRUCTIONS
### Installing Replacement Toilet

A06 → Toilet Removed

**B01** Place seal around hole in bottom / outside of tank
— Seal

**B02** Place tank on base

**B03** Insert bolts through tank and base and tighten
— Don't tighten too much or tank with crack
— Wrench

**B05** Ensure flange is tight to floor
— Remove old wax ring if necessary
— tighten or replace flange screws if necessary

**B07** Install flange bolts
— Flange bolts

**B08** Position wax ring on flange

**B09** Lower toilet onto flange
— Seat by pushing down with one hand on each side of bowl

**B10** Install washers and nuts
— Hand tighten
— Alternately tighten on each side of bowl

**B11** Install caps

**B12** Reconnect water line

**B13** Turn on water supply

**B14** Check for leaks
— No leaks detected → End
— Leak from base
— Leak from tank
— Leak from water source

Seal placed · Tank placed · Toilet assembled · Flange prepared · Flange bolts installed · Wax ring installed · Toilet lowered onto flange · Nuts installed and tightened · Caps installed · Water reconnected · Water supply turned on

TaskMap™
PROCESSES MADE EASY

to do the project. If it is the first time you have done this job, guidelines will provide step-by-step instructions of what to do and check. Complete each guideline before moving to the next step or activity.

Another factor affecting guidelines—as you can see from this example—is the skill level of individuals doing the work. The skill and experience level has a big impact on determining the level of detail and the management of guidelines in a project.

Table 3.4 shows different types of guidelines including instructions, hints, policies, procedures, instructions, business rules, and safety requirements. The level of detail in your guidelines, determines how well someone gets it right the first time. If you don't provide the supervision and the checkpoints to ensure that the guidelines are followed, you only have yourself to blame.

TABLE 3.4 *Guidelines*

| GUIDELINE | EXPLANATION | EXAMPLE |
|---|---|---|
| Instructions | Information and advice to follow for the project or task | How to assemble the toilet |
| Rules or regulations | Specific governance to follow to correctly complete the task or activity | Report and out-of-quality-range items |
| Hints | Ideas that help complete the task successfully | Shortcuts to smooth the repair process |
| Procedures | A step-by-step review of how to complete a specific task | Follow these steps to ensure that the "cake bakes" successfully |

## PUTTING IT ALL TOGETHER

So we've explored the five areas that make up the various elements within the project. The individual elements themselves are not that complex. Many involved with project management want to make it complex and confusing—I don't really know why, but they do. One factor that contributes to complexity is terminology, and that is the reason I want you to think about managing only five different things. They are all you need to consider.

Each activity or task links to the budget line item, and when combined constitute a complete process or part of the project. The budget and cost management are important to keep in mind for all activities associated with your projects.

FIGURE 3.4 *Individual Tasks*

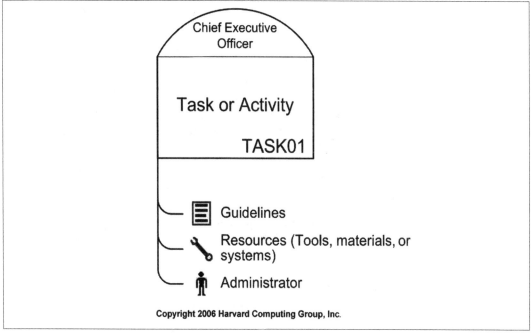

TaskMap® example courtesy Harvard Computing Group

The following chapters introduce a simple, three-stage approach to get you using these five elements effectively in the context of planning, implementing, and managing projects.

During the next three chapters you will learn how a simple, three-step process—plan, implement, and manage—will jump start and improve your project management career. These three steps will provide an effective means to keep projects under control. The three chapters explain each of these steps in detail, providing a solid and comprehensible foundation for any project in your future.

An important part of keeping our strategy simple is limiting the use of special terminology and complex frameworks. Project management is tough enough to begin with without making it more difficult with a language only *professionals* can understand. We will not render the mind numb with stages, phases, segments, criteria, and other mumbo jumbo that distract from the goal of managing your project. By concentrating on these few steps, it becomes obvious where the project stands and what needs to happen next.

> *An important part of keeping our strategy simple is limiting the use of special terminology and complex frameworks. Project management is tough enough to begin with without making it more difficult with a language only professionals can understand.*

So much is complicated in the project management world, seemingly just to keep the bar high. Professional groups focus on complex terminology and inscrutable diagrams, and professional organizations make it hard to join. As everyone is a project manager of something, a lot is gained by simplifying this charge. In my day job, I interact with hundreds of project managers every year, and the best ones understand this is a major problem and are investing heavily in methods and technologies to improve communication between their groups within the organization. *Simplify* is becoming a mantra for improving information flow, knowledge transfer, and project management across many organizations.

This book deliberately limits the use of acronyms (except by way of the intentionally miniscule glossary—for those of you who really care about them). Plain language is the hallmark of the very best in project management. Why? Because all participants understand the communication if the language is simple and the focus is on the contents of the project and not on the special handshakes or peculiar project management jargon.

*Each project begins as an idea*
*that germinates into a plan.*

In order for something to reach that first tangible stage— *the plan*—there needs to be an idea, agreement, or event. For example, consider the project of an addition to an existing home as an alternative to moving. The need for the addition requires contractors, architects, and permits, just to name a few things. The need sets everything in motion and propels the move to the first step—creating the plan.

# 4

# STEP 1: THE PLAN

*"All men seek one goal: success or happiness. The only way to achieve true success is to express yourself completely in service to society. First, have a definite, clear, practical ideal–a goal, an objective. Second, have the necessary means to achieve your ends–wisdom, money, material and methods. Third, adjust all your means to that end."*

**Aristotle**

**D**eveloping a project plan can take many forms. The simpler the project, the easier to plan; as the complexity increases, so do the variables and time required to create an effective plan. As discussed earlier, the plan is not the initial idea that germinates the project but does mark a point where a framework is needed to predict and manage project outcomes. Before getting into the details of the planning process itself, we must turn our attention to and goals and objectives.

## GOALS AND OBJECTIVES

While it may appear obvious that any plan should have clearly defined goals and objectives, the number of projects that start out without this seemingly basic platform is amazing.

Take this book, for example; the idea for the book germinated from discussions between my agent, John Willig, and me. Over the course of almost a year, we reviewed the potential for a book that would simplify and demystify project management.

Did we go directly from an idea to a project plan? No. First we had to address the marketability of such a book. Starting with clear objectives and goals that would benefit the reader, a "business case" was created for the publisher. Then we had to find which publishers would be willing to support and publish it.

This example represents exactly what has to occur in the development of any new project—and *in advance* of the planning phase. Goals and objectives are very important, as they represent the results and vision of what participants or financiers want out of the project. Many times these are not well communicated, creating confusion later in the project, particularly when conveyance of changes to goals is ineffective and results in unexpected outcomes. This creates, at a minimum, disappointment and frequently, more damaging fallout.

## Define the Goals and Objectives Up Front

Every project should have goals and objectives; and defining them up front assists dramatically with the decision-making processes in the planning phase. In fact, well-defined goals and objectives assist the planning process, as they articulate what is and is not acceptable in terms of outcomes. They also impact the management approach in all phases of the project—dependencies on available resources, budgets, and time constraints—as we will explore later.

FIGURE 4.1 *Goals and Objectives*

---

# Example of goals and objectives

➢ Reduce the number of steps and time for a particular process by 25%

➢ Cut the cost from the overall process by 30%

➢ Shorten our product development lifecycle by 15%

➢ Save at least $1m per annum in overhead costs

TaskMap™
PROCESSES MADE EASY

© 2005 Harvard Computing Group, Inc.  HARVARD

---

Courtesy Harvard Computing Group

*"We aim above the mark to hit the mark."*

Ralph Waldo Emerson

People are often confused about the difference between goals and objectives. Goals tend to be broad based and less specific than objectives. However, in many cases we use goals and objectives in a combined way that provides high-level guidance and specific measurements for what we want to achieve.

The examples in the following diagram are in this category. We can "reduce the number of steps" as a high-level goal but link them to a specific objective of 25 percent.

Depending on the type of project and the decision-making team, the preparation work, research, and time involved varies. For example, a small project might be a couple deciding to purchase a new car. A major business project example is a company's decision to develop a new product line.

The couple making the decision for the car might consider issues such as:

- Fuel economy
- Styling
- Size
- Handling
- Price
- Cost of ownership

Once established, the project manager begins to prioritize by forming goals and objectives for the project. In order for this to occur, other factors start to come into play. Budget, time, and resources are the next three areas that you have to consider for every project.

Obviously, without these constraints many projects can overrun, never finish, and even ruin the financiers or project owners. History is littered with examples; ask anyone who has done renovation, restoration, or unique building projects—they all have a story to tell. Everyone has some experience with projects that have missed the mark in various ways, so each project has to be bound by some criteria that determine its success.

In the case of the car, the budget may be constrained by the size of the car payment or cost of ownership. Therefore, vehicles with maintenance included or longer warranty periods have to be considered versus purchase price alone. Financing terms, the competitive situation in the market, and how long the owners plan to keep the car all affect how goals are determined.

In more complex situations, consultation with others may be needed to establish priorities. If these goals have not been set as starting points for the project, then they will have to be developed. An excellent way of doing this is to set up a brainstorming session.

*People are often confused about the difference between goals and objectives. Goals tend to be broad based and less specific than objectives. However, in many cases we use goals and objectives in a combined way that provides high-level guidance and specific measurements for what we want to achieve.*

## BRAINSTORMING

Over recent years, *brainstorming* has gone from a generic term to a science supported by abundant material, experts, and even software. For those of you who have not experienced a brainstorming session, you may be missing something. The idea is to extract as many ideas as you can from the collective intellect of those present at the session and then organize them into something useful.

Done well, this can be a great starting point for a new project. Executed badly, it can derail and even reduce support for whatever you are trying to achieve. Before setting up a brainstorming session, clear directions about the project's management requirements are needed before getting everyone together.

Individuals need to know that the gathering is going to be constructive and the creativity and input of those present will be required. With many hours often wasted in meetings across the world, setting up a meeting with less-than-tangible goals can often receive a lukewarm reaction. For example, *we are going to meet to see if you have any good ideas about this . . .*

It's better to start by proposing a challenge or a question that needs answering and input to encourage useful participation. In addition, remember that each person attending has a different perspective, particularly when it comes to creative ideas. In a good brainstorming session, you want ideas from the "quiet ones" as well as from those who cannot remain silent for more than a few minutes. To create this efficiently often requires the presence of an external facilitator, mainly because existing internal or operational managers often create a "staid" atmosphere, hindering "out-of-the-box" or creative thinking.

For me, creative thinking tends to come very frequently. In fact, as a manager I am not the best person to have around if everything is going smoothly, as I have a tendency to "keep adjusting the dials" looking for change, even if it is not needed. That said, there is always a mixture of personalities in any operation, making managing the mix of those present in the session important.

A few guidelines on brainstorming sessions include:

1. Make it clear that you are mining for ideas that can improve the area of operation or project that will emerge from the session—you are not judging their validity or applicability during the meeting.

2. Have a facilitator who will not intimidate participants. Staff and team members are less likely to come up with ideas if they know that the president is running the meeting and going to have his or her bias for each area. Careers can be made or lost in such circumstances.

3. Creation of a politically neutral environment is important to success. Even having a "mulligan" for the really bad ideas can make people feel at ease and more likely to open up.

4. Use paper or other neutral means as another option to capture ideas. This is useful if some participants are uncomfortable providing verbal contributions. The "quiet ones" often have great ideas.

5. Although overused, the concept of "out-of-the-box" thinking is very important, and even delivering a couple of examples can be a great icebreaker at the outset.

6. As always, set time frames, goals, and a clear agenda for the meeting.

A casual business setting can be the best way to lead others into contributing ideas of great value to an organization. Informal lunches, sporting events, and charity and fundraising programs can help cross organizational development; all offer ways for team members from diverse groups to participate. Once you have the forum for your brainstorming session established, set up the meeting. The following agenda provides some guidance. Each of these sessions has to reflect the culture of the organization and ensure the buy-in of attendees.

TABLE 4.1 *Brainstorming Agenda*

| | |
|---|---|
| **DATE:** | |
| Attendees and company: | |
| Subject: Idea generation session | |
| 10:00 AM–10:15 AM | Introductions<br>Review of the purpose of the session<br>Description of rules and tools prepared for the session |
| 10:15 AM–11:15 AM | Begin brainstorming program:<br>• Identify target areas for improvement or change<br>• Capture the ideas<br>• Organize the ideas into groups<br>• Prioritize |
| 11:15 AM–11:45 AM | Determine which ideas have the most merit<br>Discuss follow-up actions |

## Brainstorming Your Way to Goals and Objectives

The creation and development of ideas do not have to occur in a particular order, but once created they become factors that affect the decision-making process. Some may argue that brainstorming is a key part of the planning process and that generating ideas is important to successful planning—do not confuse the two areas. Providing the list of ideas helps you to prioritize your project and the criteria for success.

Therefore, the first three stages to determining goals and priorities are:

1. Development of ideas that are relevant to the project

2. Conversion of those ideas to goals

3. Creation of specific objectives from those goals

# SETTING UP THE PLAN

Now that we have goals and objectives defined, we move on to creating the plan. The first part in determining the various elements to be included is a careful dissection of the goals and objectives.

For example, our overall goal is to increase sales by 20 percent over the next fiscal year, and our specific objectives include increasing sales by 20 percent while maintaining margins at 30 percent and not increasing costs by more than 10 percent. Here it is clear that the overall goal of increasing sales will be successful only if it is within the criteria of the specific objectives. In this example, you need to ensure costs do not get out of control, or you risk adversely affecting margins and profitability. It really doesn't matter what the project is, the factors of goals and objectives always apply. If you start a project and find they are not well defined, then work this issue until they are unambiguous. It is extremely important in the early planning stages that goals and objectives are clear and that an acceptable range of flexibility on costs, budgets, and results is agreed.

*"All things are created twice. There's a mental or first creation, and a physical or second creation of all things. You have to make sure that the blueprint, the first creation, is really what you want, that you've thought everything through. Then you put it into bricks and mortar. Each day you go to the construction shed and pull out the blueprint to get marching orders for the day. You begin with the end in mind."*

Stephen R. Covey,
*The 7 Habits of Highly Effective People*

Once these high-level objectives are determined, start to decompose them into lower-level objectives. The lower-level objectives can be viewed as results or milestones and are usually captured in a sequential manner reflecting the order in which they will be completed for the specific project.

## THE MILESTONE

One term important to project management is *the milestone*. The milestone is a marker that indicates that some activity or process has been completed. In my native England, actual milestones are still visible on some highways and date back to Roman times when legions would measure their progress and ensure that they were still on the right road. Sounds good to me!

*Do not confuse milestones with project activities.* Milestones are results of something being completed, not an individual activity. Once you identify and group the correct sequence for the project, milestones provide a great framework for planning. As Table 4.2 illustrates, the milestones denote reference points in your project for the successful meeting of goals and objectives, albeit representing only a portion of the entire project. This breakdown provides us with the exact guidance we need to move to an important next step in the planning phase—the estimate. This is where we can begin adding information related to people, resources, and costs.

Once you have these organized, you will start to see what needs to happen next. The order in which it needs to happen and your milestones will represent checkpoints for your project and determine whether it is on track.

TABLE 4.2 *Milestones*

| MILESTONE | EXPLANATION |
|---|---|
| Task or activity completed | Activity completed successfully |
| Project phase completed | Project phase completed successfully |
| Project completed | Entire project completed successfully |

*Linking the milestone to specific objectives is a great practice to ensure that the milestone meets both the objective and the time line.*

# THE PROCESS

As we start the planning process, some recommend separating estimates from the plan. This does not make sense, because if you cannot accurately document the likely incurred costs, it will be unlikely that the project concludes on time or within budget. *Bottom-up* planning creates the best basis for estimating; and there is no shortcut to estimating.

Now that we have the basic measurements in place for the project steps, our next stage is to break down parts of the project and determine how they interact. Here's the magic; think about every component in your project as a separate, self-contained series of steps in a *process.*

Every project is merely a series of processes knitted together in a particular order with a particular set of dependencies. The more you understand that in project management, the fewer surprises and the more success you will have in any project you are managing.

FIGURE 4.2 *How Tasks and Activities Become Processes*

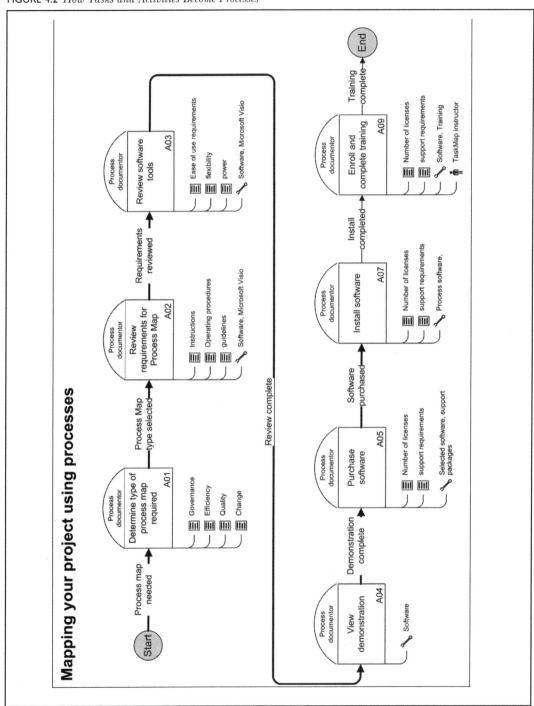

As each activity or task connects together, a process is born. As each process connects together, the overall project emerges.

By taking each of the elements, we consider how to apply them in a complete process to reach the first milestone. Activities are tasks; connect tasks together and it creates a process. Looking at project management in this way, you can digest things in smaller bites, which makes even the largest projects seem more manageable.

Creating a proposal, we can take the overall objective of creating it during a specific period of time and within a certain budget as one milestone in the overall project cycle. The objective also becomes the deliverable, ensuring that our goals and objectives are being tied to our results—an excellent project management practice.

Therefore, we begin by breaking out various elements to reach each goal, and we begin to create manageable activities.

People view activities in different ways, causing confusion around terminology. Let's break this down into more detail so it is really clear. An activity defines an action that produces results. That wasn't so hard, was it? Every activity can be broken into several components:

- The need to do the activity
- The activity itself
- What other supporting elements make up the activity—resources, guidelines, people, materials, time, and more
- The result of the activity
- Follow-up actions

For our purposes here, I would recommend that you use the word *task* for all activities. There are several reasons for that, not just personal preference. First, a task is a more precise description of an activity; second, all of the elements discussed in Chapter 3 fit neatly into a task function; and, finally, confusion is less likely among activities, tasks, and milestones.

> *If you need to provide a tutorial or lecture*
> *at the beginning of each of your meetings*
> *so people can understand your terminology,*
> *you will be on the wrong track from the get-go.*

One of the reasons for selecting the limited and clear terminology for project management is to spend more time talking about the contents and plans within the project rather than the terminology itself. Believe me, if you need to provide a tutorial or lecture at the beginning of each of your meetings so people can understand what you're saying, you will be on the wrong track from the get-go.

So the project plan starts to take shape: first, the project goals and objectives, and then the high-level framework of the order of those objectives, representing attainable milestones in the project plan. Finally, we document these as processes that represent a series of tasks and their results to meet those milestones.

Once at this stage, we are ready to start adding the real details to our project plan. Using the milestones, we begin by initially identifying the time line required to achieve the project plan, and ensuring that it meets the goals laid out in the beginning of the project. Having enough detail in these milestones makes it easier to translate these to specific actions in the project plan.

For example, in preparing to attend a trade show, we need to make sure that all preparation, brochures, travel booking, staff briefing, and material purchasing occur before walking in and setting up our booth. Creating a logical sequence of actions and events in the project plan illuminates how this is going to occur.

TABLE 4.3 *Simplified Terminology*

| TERM | EXPLANATION | ALSO KNOWN AS (AKA) |
|---|---|---|
| Activity or Tasks | Actions or discrete events within a project | Actions, steps |
| Goals | High-level description of desired results from the project | Sometimes confused with objectives and targets |
| Objectives | A detailed description of a specific result desired from the project | Sometimes confused with goals and targets |
| Results | Outcomes | Outcomes, consequences |
| Processes | A series of activities linked together in a logical sequence as required by the project plan | Subprocesses, stages, or project phases |
| Procedures | A process packaged into a specific set of directives to be followed for a project | Often confused with guidelines or instructions; actual procedures have guidance plus the activities to meet the requirements |
| Budget | An approved cost estimate for the project | Cost schedule, financial plan |
| Decisions | Determinations made within the project | Outcomes, results |
| Phase or Stage | A section of a large project broken into smaller pieces | Segment or subproject |
| Schedule | Time line for the project or project activities | Timetable, time-based plan |
| Milestones | A measurable point in the schedule with specific results and outcomes | Deliverables, dates |

FIGURE 4.3 *High-Level Budget with Phases and Tasks Noted*

| Phase | Task | Time | Consultant Type | | | Rate | | | Sub-Totals | Totals |
|---|---|---|---|---|---|---|---|---|---|---|
| | | | Res. | EP | BS | Res. | EP | BS | | |
| 1 | **KM Technology Awareness** | | | | | | | | | |
| | Delivery in Cairo | | 1 | 1 | | 1200 | 2200 | 3300 | 3400 | 3400 |
| | Development costs and research | | | | | | | | | |
| | KM overview and introduction | | 1 | | | 1200 | 2200 | 3300 | 1200 | 1200 |
| | How to use KM to benefit your operation | | 1 | | | 1200 | 2200 | 3300 | 1200 | 1200 |
| | Benefits and applications (case studies) | | 1 | | | 1200 | 2200 | 3300 | 1200 | 1200 |
| | Integrating KM with other environments | | 0.5 | | | 1200 | 2200 | 3300 | 600 | 600 |
| | Developing Return on Investment model | | 0.5 | | | 1200 | 2200 | 3300 | 600 | 600 |
| | How to introduce KM to your firm | | 0.5 | | | 1200 | 2200 | 3300 | 600 | 600 |
| | Documentation | | 1 | | | 1200 | 2200 | 3300 | 1200 | 1200 |
| | Total days | 7.5 | 6.5 | 1 | | | | | Total = | $10,000 |
| | Total hours | | 52 | 8 | | | | | | |
| | Development costs | $6,600 | | | | | | | Grand Total | $10,000 |

Once we identify milestones, we can then examine what process is required to meet them, for example, planning for the trade show (see Figure 4.4).

By examining each detail, we can start capturing the additional information required to successfully complete this part of the project—the process in hand. In fact, this process is just one piece of the project; consider the entire project as a completed jigsaw puzzle and each piece as a process that, when combined, connects it.

The next logical step is to add the elements we identified in Chapter 3 in as much detail as it is relevant for the plan. The resources required: trade show manual, trade show reports, event Web site, sales reports, travel company, literature layout, and so on. Costs involved for these resources should also be captured.

FIGURE 4.4 *Trade Show Preparation*

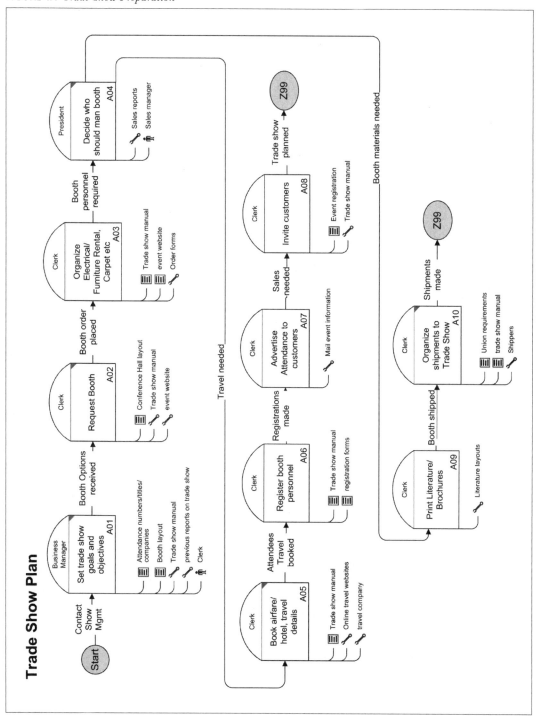

Also acquire instructions, where relevant, to identify the order in which these tasks should be completed and any other procedures to be followed that might be relevant. Looking at things at this level of detail drives participants to understand the various elements of each project in as much detail as is important to you as the project manager and the team. The customer is expecting you to deliver.

## WHAT THE PLAN LOOKS LIKE

So, what should a project plan look like? Well it might be a list (as illustrated previously), a spreadsheet, a table, or other various types of visual presentation.

The spreadsheet can represent an excellent lowest common denominator to create your project plan for the following reasons:

- Spreadsheets illustrate step-by-step milestones quickly and efficiently.

- Spreadsheets allow clear, simple enumeration of milestones and tasks.

- Inserting additional information regarding costs to tasks and associated elements such as tools, systems, and materials is easy.

- Accessibility; most people have access to a spreadsheet, even if they do not have access to dedicated project management software such as Microsoft Project, Primerva, and other programs.

- It is relatively easy to hide additional detail in a spreadsheet by either using pivot tools or controlling display options.

Now don't get me wrong; there are times when using a dedicated project management system will have benefits. However, following the philosophy of this book, which is to simplify project management, building your plan in a tool that pretty much everyone has access to improves communication, makes it easier for reviewers and participants to make changes, and makes it simple to keep this information up-to-date.

One of the major problems in many project management planning phases is the creation of the estimate in a system that no one can access. This means generating reports in order to distribute information about the project plan and making it much more difficult to keep that information up-to-date. Once a project starts, the participants obviously have a huge impact on whether things finish on time and within budget, and so limiting their access to the tools that reflect these changes creates an unnecessary barrier. The spreadsheet breaks down this barrier and promotes communication.

Once we enter the plan information, we can add additional details to start the estimate. Looking at the rows and columns of the spreadsheet in Figure 4.5, you can see where time, budget, resources, guidelines, and roles play their parts in creating an accurate estimate. The plan is starting to take shape, and once we have enough information, the probable duration and cost levels of the project begin emerging. We can then determine the accuracy of our plan and examine some of the risk areas before finalizing.

At this estimating and planning stage, we must examine a few more things before starting the project. These include dependencies, risk factors, and budget.

FIGURE 4.5 *Spreadsheet Sample*

| | | K32 | | | | | | | | | | |
|---|---|---|---|---|---|---|---|---|---|---|---|---|
| | A | B | C | E | F | G | H | I | J | K | L | M |
| 4 | | EP Rate | 2200 | | | | | | | | | |
| 5 | | Business Strategy Rate | 3300 | | | | | | | | | |
| 6 | | Course attendance up to 20 | | | | | | | | | | |
| 7 | | | | Consultant Type | | | Rate | | | | | |
| 8 | Phase | Task | Time | Res. | EP | BS | Res. | EP | BS | Sub-Totals | Totals | |
| 9 | 1 | Procurement guide | | | | | | | | | | |
| 10 | | Delivery in Cairo (2 days) | | 1 | 2 | | 1200 | 2200 | 3300 | 5600 | 5600 | |
| 11 | | Development costs and research | | | | | 1200 | 2200 | 3300 | 0 | 0 | |
| 12 | | Reducing the risk of IT purchases | | | | | 1200 | 2200 | 3300 | 1800 | 1800 | |
| 13 | | **Developing and releasing an RFP** | | | | | 1200 | 2200 | 3300 | 1200 | 1200 | |
| 14 | | Responding to an RFP | | | | | 1200 | 2200 | 3300 | 900 | 900 | |
| 15 | | **Developing Return on Investment model** | | | | | 1200 | 2200 | 3300 | 2300 | 2300 | |
| 16 | | Vendor selection criteria | | | | | 1200 | 2200 | 3300 | 300 | 300 | |
| 17 | | **Fixed price or time and materials** | | | | | 1200 | 2200 | 3300 | 1200 | 1200 | |
| 18 | | Issuing and managing the contract and project | | | | | 1200 | 2200 | 3300 | 600 | 600 | |
| 19 | | **Signing off on deliverables** | | | | | 1200 | 2200 | 3300 | 1200 | 1200 | |
| 20 | | Resolving contract issues (simple to arbitration) | | | | | 1200 | 2200 | 3300 | 600 | 600 | |
| 21 | | Documentation of courseware | | | | | 1200 | 2200 | 3300 | 4800 | 4800 | |
| 24 | | Total days | 15 | 12.5 | 2.5 | | | | | Total = | $20,500 | |
| 25 | | Total hours | | 100 | 20 | | | | | | | |
| 27 | | **Bold sections have workshop exercises involved** | | | | | | | | Grand Total | $20,500 | |
| 29 | | Development costs | $14,900 | | | | | | | | | |

Comment box:

> Mikec:
> introduction to step by step process to determine needs and requirements for buyers. Includes Technology Awareness, issues of process change, Return on Investment, RFI, RFP stages, down to making the decisions. (about a 1.5 hr intro to the process)

# DEPENDENCIES

Dependencies are really quite simple. Does one thing have to happen successfully before moving to the next process or starting the work toward the next milestone? Tiling cannot start in the bathroom until work on the subfloor finishes. Therefore we have a dependency to lay the subfloor before laying tile on the floor.

When reviewing the project plan, it may be obvious that tasks need to happen in a certain order. At other times it may be less obvious. Once laid out, it becomes easier to determine whether dependencies are present among the milestones. For many projects these things are not very complex to figure out.

TABLE 4.4 *Dependencies*

| DEPENDENCIES | EXPLANATION |
|---|---|
| Prior task | Successful completion of the previous task or activity is required. |
| Approvals | Some approval is required before the next activity or stage can commence. |
| Budget overrun | Part of the project has or is likely to run over budget; revisions and changes will need approval before going forward. |
| Change in goals, objectives, or scope | Dependencies are likely to change if there are any changes in scope, objectives, or goals. |

In other cases, task decisions may require managing around availability of resources and other elements.

A good example of a project that is typically organized around costs and availability of resources and budget is a movie. It is rare that a movie is shot starting at the beginning and concluding at the end. The reason is the cost associated with locations, crews, and special effects, all of which affect the filming order of the project. This additional factor of dependencies and the relationship to costs affects the logical order being different from the actual order to run the project.

# RISKS

Risks are measurable in lots of different ways. There are three levels of risks associated with any project.

1. The risk of an incomplete project
2. The risk going over budget or not being complete within the time frame
3. The risk of partial failure

All of these are bad, of course, but some are deadly. Incomplete projects or going over budget in a big way can be career limiting, cost millions, and create legal liabilities and repercussions in the end. The risks associated with the first two levels need to be factored at the planning and estimating stage.

In general, the risk associated with the project and the potential repercussions increase dramatically with size, complexity, and time associated with completion. In Boston, the tunnel project to submerge the freeways through the city is an example of a project completely out of control from both time frame and cost perspectives. Initial estimates in the two billion-dollar range proved to be inaccurate, to an order of magnitude. The project management bill alone for this program has exceeded $100 million. Large projects like this have huge technical complexity, massive government regulation, and inconsistent management; add in a long period for implementation, and you have all the ingredients for failure. While the results may have some long-term benefits to the commuter, it is obvious that the goals, objectives, milestones, and budget were not well planned, estimated, or managed.

Fortunately, most of us will not have to manage anything like "The Big Dig" in Boston. However, we can learn some of the basics of planning and risk management and their implications in the initial estimate.

An important part of any project is a high comfort level with partners who provide resources and people to meet its goals. One example might be selecting a software system as your project; this means evaluating vendors, purchase costs, maintenance overhead, training, reliability, and suitability for purpose, all having an effect on the selection criteria. This translates directly to risk factors, and for our purposes we recommend a five-point system to rate risks.

On this scale, five is very high and one is very low. Our goal will be to have the lowest risks on components of the project that either are high cost or have a serious dependency that will affect your outcome.

Highest risk factors can be assigned to an overall process within the project milestone resulting from it. Once identified, begin determining what reduces these risks, or if you are not sure, add more detail to see where the greatest risk lies.

Suppliers, roles, resources, material availability, and even the weather can add to risk factors. As the project manager, you have the responsibility for the estimate, so you have to decide where risks reside and, in the absence of relevant experience, which risk factors require additional resources for you to assess and deal with.

The construction industry may necessitate contracting an architect or quantity surveyor to assist with this work. The engineering sector may call for a production engineer or industrial designer. The bottom line: If additional resources are required to assess risks, it is better to get them in early—particularly if the project scope is outside existing subject matter expertise, experience, or comfort levels.

## BUDGET

Last but not least on the checklist for estimating is the budget. As discussed earlier, no matter how great the project plan we have, the project will not fly if our budget is wrong because it is not affordable.

Sometimes, the budget can be come a great source of creativity. For example, consider a project where the goals are

FIGURE 4.6 *Budget Information Spreadsheet*

| | E | F | G |
|---|---|---|---|
| **Development Estimate** | | | |
| | | | |
| Development costs | | # trainees | |
| CRM | $ 10,200.00 | | |
| SCM | $ 12,000.00 | | |
| KM | $ 6,600.00 | | |
| Buying and selling IT systems | $ 14,900.00 | | Average cost/student course |
| | | | |
| | | | |
| Total | $ 43,700.00 | | |
| | | | |
| Delivery costs | | | |
| | | | |
| CRM | $ 6,800.00 | | |
| SCM | $ 6,800.00 | | |
| KM | $ 6,800.00 | | |
| Buying and selling IT systems | $ 11,200.00 | | |
| | | | |
| Deliver costs for 2 week session | $ 31,600.00 | | |
| | | | |
| With single 2 weeks session del | $ 75,300.00 | 160 | $ 470.63 |
| | | | |
| With 2 deliveries total cost | $106,900.00 | 320 | $ 334.06 |
| | | | |
| With 3 deliveries total cost | $138,500.00 | 640 | $ 216.41 |
| | | | |
| With 4 deliveries total cost | $170,100.00 | 1280 | $ 132.89 |

clear and the milestones laid out but the proposed plan is obviously not affordable. When faced with this situation, you have other alternatives to consider, including

1. reducing the scope of the project;

2. outsourcing components to the most cost-effective supplier or partner; or

3. reducing the quality of the components or dramatically changing the plan.

Sometimes, budgetary problems can cause project managers and their teams to come up with very innovative solutions. As a motorcycle enthusiast, I have found that many budget-driven decisions have improved the quality of motorcycle products, while saving manufacturing costs and material costs and reducing maintenance costs. Thirty years ago, most motorcycles had a traditional tubular frame wherein the engine resided. Today, almost all motorcycles use the engine as a stressed member of the frame, reducing weight and cost and improving maintainability. Design changes have the benefits of saving money and improving the performance at the same time. If there had never been any price pressure, perhaps the designer would not have considered such a radical change. So if estimates are too high, examine not only reducing scope or existing costs, but also consider how things might be different.

Once the estimate and plan are complete, the ingredients are in place for the next phase: implementing the plan.

# 5

# STEP 2: IMPLEMENT

**A**s the plan takes shape, we are ready to move to the next stage: implementing the plan. During this step, use the information gathered and documented in the planning phase to start the project. At this point you should have in place

1. the Project Plan (as agreed from Step 1); and
2. an agreement of budget and management approval to move to implementation stage.

This sounds obvious, right? Ensuring that the approval is in place, however, has bitten many an inexperienced manager; also, the approval should be in writing. As Jack Warner (of Warner Brothers fame) once quipped, "A verbal contract is not worth the paper it's written on."

Before the project is started, care should be taken to finalize key aspects of the plan that are often missed.

# ALMOST READY TO GO

Before the project starts, some additional details—the final steps—need to be taken care of before kicking off the project. This almost-ready phase is often missed. As there are usually lapses in time between planning and implementation, important items can fall through the cracks. To ensure that the project does not suffer from these mistakes, take the following actions.

## Review the Goals and Objectives, and Gain Affirmation

During the planning step, we reviewed the importance of linking goals and objectives in detail. Ensuring that all parties are on the same page and that they clearly understand the goals and objectives and how they will create milestones is crucial.

Take the time to review each goal and its supporting objectives with everyone involved. Each of these objectives should translate to specific actions from project participants. The impact of poorly defined goals and objectives should not be underestimated. During every project, there may be cases where the method or means of reaching milestones may change. While this might be acceptable—or even encouraged—reaching the wrong destination or results is not. Therefore, the relationship between goals, objectives, and milestones is vital.

Participants need to understand that changes in method or means may be acceptable, but changes in results are not. This creates a desire to link results with goals and objectives.

Milestones become a pure measuring post, indicating where we should be at a given point in the project.

One advantage of adding this additional review point as you begin to implement the project is to clear up these misunderstandings before they start becoming part of the project outcome. This is the time to add the detail, be more specific, sharpen the vision, and remove any gray areas from the program. Consider the links between goals, objectives, and milestones illustrated here:

1. The goal is to increase sales by 20 percent.
2. The objectives are to do so by increasing staff by only 10 and overhead by 15 percent within one year.
3. The milestone will be increasing sales by 20 percent with overhead increased by a maximum of 15 percent, thereby maintaining margins within the 12-month period.

The goals and objectives drive the requirements for the milestone. The milestone documents the result and when it should occur. Understanding this relationship will pay huge dividends as the project gets started.

Another reason for this review is to ensure time lines are in sync with original agreements in the planning stage. Many involved in projects seem willing to commit to dates at the planning step, but then, when the rubber hits the road, want to reconsider. Ensuring buy-in occurs at this point is an excellent practice.

*Participants need to understand that changes*
*in method or means may be acceptable,*
*but changes in results are not.*

## Selecting Vendors and Partners

Depending on the project type, it is possible that outside suppliers, vendors, or partners will be involved. As discussed during the planning stage, it is critical that these selection decisions are exemplary, as they will have a significant impact on the potential success of your project.

*"Alone we can do so little;*
*together we can do so much."*

Helen Keller

Figuring out how to choose the right vendors, suppliers, and partners is often the mark of an excellent project manager. Of course the right ones help considerably in the creation of the very best of results and deal with the nasty problems and difficulties that occur once the project is under way. In the absence of experience in this area, fortunately there is a series of actions to follow that reduce the potential for making poor choices.

An important aspect of selecting any partner or supplier is the synergy and empathy felt during the selection process. It is necessary to deal with this issue up front, as obviously it is a greater delight to deal with those we like and feel we will enjoy working with. However, making decisions on this basis can also cause problems. If other factors such as price, time frame, and quality are not so important, you might find yourself doing business with someone you like but with less-than-perfect results.

*"The Law of Win/Win says,*
*'Let's not do it your way or my way;*
*let's do it the best way.'"*

Greg Anderson, *The 22 Non-Negotiable*
*Laws of Wellness: Take Your Health Into Your*
*Own Hands to Feel, Think, and Live Better*
*Than You Ever Thought Possible*

The bottom line is that no one wants to do business with someone who is a pain to deal with, but producing the desired results has to be the priority. If not, the project will not meet its goal: successful delivery—on time and on budget.

When selecting vendors and partners, take the following steps:

1. Measure the cost associated with the development of the relationship.

2. Determine the margin and cost of goods from the partnerships.

3. Review the reengineering costs associated with the partner relationships.

4. Consider additional costs for marketing, sales, training, management, and maintenance of the relationship.

5. On a distribution partnership project, agree on metrics and goals for the sale of goods and supporting costs.

The converse of this issue is also true. Once we find partners and suppliers who have delivered the goods within the project criteria, they will be invited back to many projects under our control. The risk reduction factor of dealing with known entities and effective working relationships is a great way of cutting risk out of the project from the start.

One factor deserving consideration that is hard to quantify but is often a gut-level feeling is the trust factor. While some of this can be checked through references and the like, if a feeling of distrust is there from the beginning, then leave well enough alone. Some of my best decisions in project management have been *not* to work with an individual or organization. Likewise, some of the worst occurred by ignoring that certain gut feeling. What follows in terms of selection criteria can be measured and quantified, but the trust factor comes down to a personal decision. It must be made based on a judgment of how you are going to be treated.

> *Some of my best decisions in project*
> *management have been* not *to work*
> *with an individual or organization.*

An excellent example occurred recently at our firm when we made a selection to purchase some software through the Internet. The research indicated that one firm had the same product at 20 percent less than a rival that we had done business with previously. Bear in mind that all of these firms are offering essentially the same product and delivering over the Web.

We made the decision to buy from the 20-percent-less vendor and see what its service was like. The product was not expensive—less than $100—and the order placed. Then the problems started. First, the vendor did supply the discount coupon, and the check-out price did not reflect the discount, which should have been a red flag immediately. Once we received e-mail confirmation, it turned out the vendor does not deliver the product immediately and electronically as our previous supplier had done.

The next step was to send an e-mail to the vendor's support desk, which had an individual's e-mail address—red flag number two. The good news was that we received a response within minutes. The bad news was the response itself. (See Figure 5.1).

FIGURE 5.1 *E-mail Response*

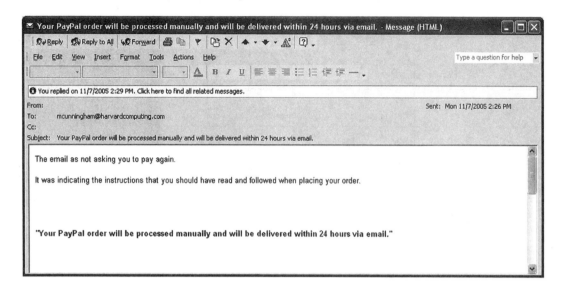

So we assumed that this was not really what was intended, and a follow-up e-mail was sent indicating that this was not the ideal way to treat a customer. Finally, we received another e-mail along with two refunds to our account—one for the discount that should have been applied in the first place and the second for the balance. There were no explanations, no apologies; just a comment that "we don't need the business that bad". Within an hour our firm returned to the original supplier, paid 20 percent more for the product, and received it within minutes. Moral of the story: Stick with your existing suppliers, and if they are not competitive, call them and ask them if they can meet the other's price. In this example, we wasted time and energy dealing with a vendor who could not care less about its customers. Imagine if these guys were important in your project supply chain.

Table 5.1 illustrates factors most likely to have an effect on your decision. These require careful consideration for even

TABLE 5.1 *Partner Research Rating Card*

| FACTOR | Rating Partner 1 | Rating Partner 2 | Rating Partner 3 | Rating Partner 4 | Rating Partner 5 | Rating Partner 6 | Rating Partner 7 | Rating Partner 8 | Rating Partner 9 | Rating Partner 10 | Rating Partner 11 | Rating Partner 12 |
|---|---|---|---|---|---|---|---|---|---|---|---|---|
| Goals | | | | | | | | | | | | |
| Vision | | | | | | | | | | | | |
| Value matching | | | | | | | | | | | | |
| Culture | | | | | | | | | | | | |
| Communication | | | | | | | | | | | | |
| Skills | | | | | | | | | | | | |
| Technology compatibility | | | | | | | | | | | | |
| Market goals | | | | | | | | | | | | |
| Industry experience | | | | | | | | | | | | |
| Process compatibility | | | | | | | | | | | | |
| Geographic location | | | | | | | | | | | | |

Source: *Partners.com* by Michael J. Cunningham. Courtesy Perseus Books.

the smallest project. The list of areas is not in any particular order—all are important.

*Price* will obviously be an important area to ensure your vendor is meeting budgetary requirements. Price has a number of dimensions that are important, such as delivery time frames, quality standards, and terms. Depending on how the project is organized, you may need to pay for deliverables in advance of shipment, partial payments up front, or special-order requirements. Some customers may be more willing than others to accept these different terms. So the actual price of a line item may not be as simple as it first appears.

Whatever the characteristics, make sure that you and your vendor understand what is expected and that it meets standard payment terms for your organization or ones that are acceptable to you.

*References* cannot be underestimated, particularly in this case. These are important for vendors and suppliers that are new to you, even when dealing with a supply of what appears to be a commodity product. The earlier example of purchasing Web-based software illustrates how easy it is to make a poor decision. When checking references, make sure that they are relevant to your project. For example, if you are selecting a partner based on subject matter expertise in a particular industry, make sure the references you receive are from that area.

This is particularly important when outsourcing or subcontracting components of a project. Check the references for the most important factors in the project at hand. These might be time limits, requirements to stay within budget, customer satisfaction, or flexibility. Again, depending on the characteristics of the project, your reference checks should be modified accordingly.

*Quality* is often misunderstood, particularly by subcontracted suppliers and outsourcing firms. If your project has a significant component that requires the subcontracted supplier to deliver to specific quality standards, make sure everything is documented, checked, and agreed upon in advance. Misunderstandings regarding quality can have huge implications, not just on the deliverables being below standard, but

then there is the remedial action that has to be taken to resolve the problem.

In the case of an engineering project, this could result in
recalls, increased expenses to the field maintenance, and in
the worst case even legal repercussions. If there are safety vi-
olations, you could require your suppliers to meet specific
standards that would have an impact on your project. Then
you need a contract that would cover these issues in advance.

Quality also has a very close relationship with cost. Suppliers that focus on providing higher-quality goods and services
tend to have lower maintenance and failure cost. See the earlier example of a car purchase decision in Chapter 4. The
trade-offs between quality, maintenance, and price warrant
consideration.

Timing is also an important factor when selecting vendors
and suppliers. Make sure you allow enough time within the
schedule for them to deliver. Vendor or supplier workloads or
materials' inventory may have changed since when you began
planning your project. For this reason, checking and factoring
in variables are very useful.

Consider confirming the time frames for deliverables to
be mandatory. In addition, also check any dependencies affecting differing suppliers.

The risk assessment model discussed in the planning
phase should be used here. It's always a good idea to have
more than one supplier or vendor in mind. Keep in your network and on your radar those that were not successful on this
particular bid. Doing so gives you the opportunity of introducing them into this or future projects should the need arise.

Using a scoring system, where one represents very low risk
and five represents very high, rate each of the variables we discussed regarding suppliers. Figure 5.3 illustrates such a
rating.

FIGURE 5.2 *Risk Assessment Factors*

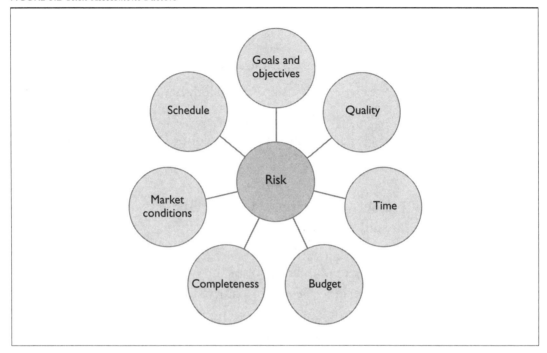

It is possible that after reviewing your supplier and vendor selection and rating outcomes that problems exist that need addressing before the project starts. These might be budgetary time lines or quality. Regardless of the source, actions will need to be determined before the project is under way.

FIGURE 5.3 *Vendor/Supplier Rating System*

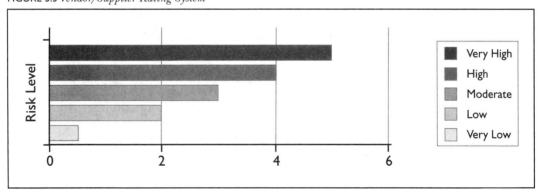

A few other items may determine selection of partners, including these:

1. Has the time frame changed?

2. Have requirements changed that might affect your selection of partner?

3. Have customer pricing requirements or market conditions changed?

Determine the impact of all of these issues on your current plan and vendor selection.

One final factor, which can be particularly important if your project plan is a proposal to win business, is experience. The experience levels in your team increase the confidence factors of your prospective client, thereby increasing the potential to win the project.

> *". . . show me that it is possible–*
> *show me your achievement–*
> *and the knowledge will give me courage for mine."*
>
> Ayn Rand, The Fountainhead

*Contracts* are important elements in dealing with vendors and suppliers. Good suppliers will insist on them, as they protect their business as well as clarify the requirements. Good contracts have the following characteristics:

- Written in plain language, devoid of ambiguity

- Clearly illustrate the requirements of products and services

- Contain details of deliverables, including materials, labor, costs

- Show the payment schedule and payment terms
- Display time lines
- Show penalties and bonuses (if applicable)
- Explain legal terms

At times, the legal terms can make up the bulk of an agreement. Some firms and organizations have standard terms they wish to apply, and large organizations have contracts and purchasing departments to screen new suppliers and contracts before projects are started with new vendors. Depending on the scope of the project and application, this may take time and should factor in any changes in time lines for your plan.

Once we've reached the conclusions regarding our vendors, we are ready to move to the next phase—starting the project.

# STARTING UP THE PROJECT

All right, so we have a plan, we selected our vendors, everyone has agreed, and we're ready to go. The first stage is to communicate each of the project elements to those involved.

## Communicating During Start-Up

For first-time project managers, it's a good idea to communicate how the project is going to be implemented along with high-level criteria before getting right into the details.

FIGURE 5.4 *Start-up Requirements*

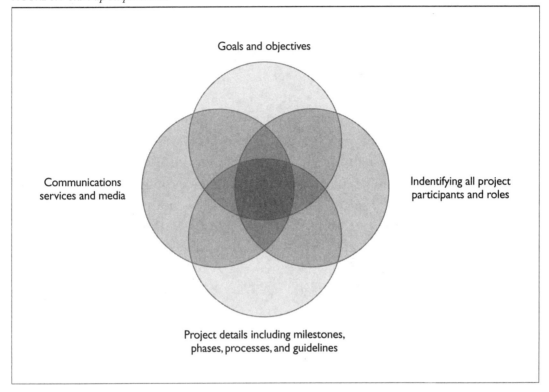

Goals and objectives

Communications
services and media

Indentifying all project
participants and roles

Project details including milestones,
phases, processes, and guidelines

This first stage should include communicating milestones, deliverables, penalties and rewards, measurement criteria, and what tools will be used to communicate with the team.

These may vary according to location, time zones, and industry and personal preferences.

The tools selected are important because everyone involved needs to see what their roles, actions, and deliverables are, and when they will be required. Recommended tools include:

- Microsoft Word or equivalent
- Microsoft Excel or equivalent
- Microsoft PowerPoint or equivalent

- E-mail program
- Internet access and a browser
- Adobe® Acrobat® reader

Consider this list a minimum for most projects today. E-mail is probably the most important, along with a telephone connection; however, it is possible to manage projects across long distances using e-mail and the above programs without a telephone connection. Microsoft Office® products are recommended because of their general availability; and even alternative solutions, such as StarOffice and Corel® Office, provide compatible formats.

Using a word-processing system such as Microsoft Word is not only advantageous because it is a common desktop tool to distribute information about the project, but also because it is useful when it comes to change management. The change control features in the product can be used to

- keep a record of changes in the project,
- provide others' input during the program, and
- distribute new versions of the implementation plan or schedule.

More sophisticated users can also utilize the Table of Contents feature to build a list of steps in the project plan. Users can create bookmarks in Excel, Word, and PowerPoint information pointers, linking important elements of the plan and activities for redistribution. This creates the equivalent of hyperlinks to relevant areas of your project plan and supporting documents.

FIGURE 5.5 *Project Outline*

## 2. Project Outline

### Project Methodology and Plan

To accomplish this project Harvard Computing Group will work with ABC Company to develop a questionnaire that will be used to conduct up to 6 interviews in each of three target market segments – service providers, enterprise customers and e-businesses. In each segment, we expect to conduct one interview face-to-face and the remainder via telephone. Tad Witkowicz or someone else from ABC Company may choose to attend a subset of the interviews.

The interviews will include questions about interviewees' performance management requirements, product feature requests and the urgency of demand for performance management products. We will also include questions designed to assess the value propositions to which potential buyers will respond and the degree to which ROI justification is required for purchases of this type. Further, we will attempt to identify who makes the buying decision for this type of product in the companies in the three target markets.

A key to the success of this project is the quality and relevance of the people with whom we are able to conduct interviews. Harvard Computing Group will work with ABC Company to identify the best candidates.

HCG will also work with ABC Company' current sales force to understand how they are 80-prospecting and selling today. Our analysis of current sales efforts, combined with information gleaned from the interviews will allow us to make recommendations for the best candidate channel partners for ABC Company' renewed sales efforts following the completion of this project.

### Anticipated Deliverables

Deliverable and due dates in the table below are subject to mutual agreement between ABC Company and Harvard Computing Group. The anticipated delivery dates are contingent upon HCG starting work toward the end of the week of 22 October 2005. A later start date will cause delivery dates to move out accordingly.

| Deliverable | Anticipated Delivery Date |
|---|---|
| Preliminary interview questionnaire | 2 November 2005 |
| Final interview questionnaire | 8 November 2005 |
| Identify interview candidates | 7 November 2005 |
| Attend ABC Company sales meetings | As required |

For projects that are business based, it would also be useful to have

- a Web-conferencing service, and
- an interim, but available, online project management site or location.

FIGURE 5.6 *Change Control Features*

## 2. Project Outline

### Project Methodology and Plan

To accomplish this project Harvard Computing Group will work with ABC Company to develop a questionnaire that will be used to conduct up to 6 interviews in each of three target market segments – service providers, enterprise customers and e-businesses. In each segment, we expect to conduct one interview face-to-face and the remainder via telephone. or someone else from ABC Company may choose to attend a subset of the interviews.

[Formatted: Font col...]

The interviews will include questions about interviewees' performance management requirements, product feature requests and the urgency of demand for performance management products. We will also include questions designed to assess the value propositions to which potential buyers will respond and the degree to which ROI justification is required for purchases of this type. Further, we will attempt to identify who makes the buying decision for this type of product in the companies in the three target markets.

A key to the success of this project is the quality and relevance of the people with whom we are able to conduct interviews. Harvard Computing Group will work with ABC Company to identify the best candidates. New changes to be added here.

HCG will also work with ABC Company' current sales force to understand how they are 80- prospecting and selling today. Our analysis of current sales efforts, combined with information gleaned from the interviews will allow us to make recommendations for the best candidate channel partners for ABC Company' renewed sales efforts following the completion of this project.

### Anticipated Deliverables

Deliverable and due dates in the table below are subject to mutual agreement between ABC Company and Harvard Computing Group. The anticipated delivery dates are contingent upon HCG starting work toward the end of the week of 22 October 2005. A later start date will cause delivery dates to move out accordingly.

| Deliverable | Anticipated Delivery Date |
|---|---|
| Preliminary interview questionnaire | 2 November 2005 |
| Final interview questionnaire | 8 December 2005 |
| Identify interview candidates | 7 November 2005 |

[Deleted: November]

If the members of your team are spread out, as is often the case, then Web conferencing and a single location to keep project information is a low-cost and effective means of communications. Web conferencing services offer the benefits of information sharing in "real time," where changes to project details are reviewable online. Other online services can be a great way to create a "virtual project office" to handle information related to the schedule, project documents, and changes.

FIGURE 5.7 *Using Bookmarks*

http://harvardcomputing.webexone.com/login.asp?loc=&link=

http://www.yale.edu/lawweb/avalon/states/mass04.htm

http://64.233.161.104/search?q=cache:Q0Ekl0rMapYJ:www.bechtel.com/pdf/
Big%2520Dig%2520Globe%2520reply.pdf+big+dig+contract+documents&hl=en&clie
nt=netscape-pp

The firm I work for uses such a service for software development projects. Many systems now provide bulletin boards, chat
services, document repositories, and calendars, all of which are
useful in keeping a project on track. More important, most of
these services are now affordable, often costing only a few hun-
dred dollars per month to provide the equivalent of thousands
of dollars of software and custom development.

Obviously, the sophistication of your communication systems and requirements will vary according to your needs. You
will note that I do not suggest that everyone on the team has a
dedicated project management software package. For the majority, many will have dedicated packages in the hands of specialist project managers or estimators.

For the most part, templates or subsets of the "entire picture" being handled by a project management system can hold
much of the project information. As there are entire books
dedicated to the selection of dedicated project management
software, I will not attempt to cover that topic here. If you are
just getting started and need a system to provide estimating
and basic project management, I would suggest that you consider Microsoft Project. This is the most popular product on
the market but still has a significant learning curve.

FIGURE 5.8 *Webex Online Office System*

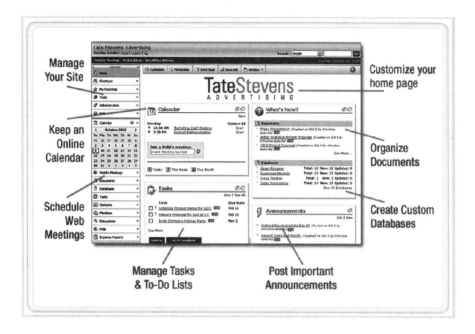

FIGURE 5.9 *Microsoft Online Meeting Product*

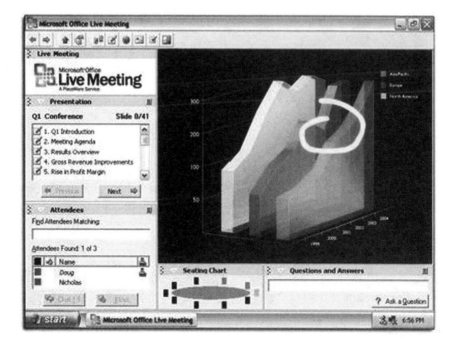

## Setting Up Meetings, Milestones, and More

Preparing for the first meeting in the project can be intimidating. Therefore it is important that your preparation be excellent so that agreements, buy-ins, changes, and the beginning of the management process will run smoothly. A lack of preparation will cause the opposite effect and create, at the very least, a false start for the project.

In setting up the first meeting it is vital to establish and affirm quality and delivery guidelines, milestones, and time lines for tasks within the project; also, to assign roles to each involved.

The kickoff meeting should have the ingredients of our discussion earlier in the book about meeting planning skills. It should also address all of the following questions and issues:

- Who should attend and what are their roles?
- What are the objectives and goals of the project?
- How will they be measured?
- What are the milestones and deliverables from each stage?
- Where are the risks and how are they going to be mitigated?
- How will the project be managed?
- Discussions and actions for the next stages

Depending on the size of the project, it may be important to release much of the background information in advance of the meeting. This allows enough time for team members to review it before the kickoff session. The last thing you need is a continuous line of questioning on areas that are answered in the plan. This way you can concentrate on the actions and issues when the project team is assembled.

Another factor with this meeting is the issue of the cost of team members being present. Larger projects could have upwards of 10–30 individuals in attendance. Making good use of their time will gain kudos; wasting it creates the reverse effect.

In getting rolling, it is also very important to emphasize quality criteria and delivery guidelines. This helps to set the bar for what is important for the project. Having to redo elements of a project because some of the tasks were not completed to a satisfactory level is very commonplace. Even if penalties or fixed-cost elements provide some protection here, missing a critical deadline may throw off the whole thing.

For example, if you do not get the foundation in place and the framing of a house completed in time for the permafrost to begin, in northern climes it might delay building until the spring. Many issues could then be affected as a result, including increased labor costs the following spring, unavailable labor, and a schedule that is now behind.

## Remote Control

One way to ensure buy-in for the project is to transfer goals and responsibilities during the kickoff meeting. Make it clear who is responsible for each task and gain acceptance during the meeting. This is an example of where relinquishing control to others in the team will help *you* gain more control of the outcome. We can effectively manage many projects outside of our subject matter expertise or skills using this technique.

Do not think of this as an abandonment of responsibility; rather, it is the opposite. Getting others to become responsible for "their part of the puzzle" translates the requirements of the project to their territory. It is then up to you to ensure that they stay on track, but more on that topic in the management step coming up in the next chapter.

> *Make it clear who is responsible for each*
> *task and gain acceptance during the project*
> *meeting. This is an example of where*
> *relinquishing control to others in the team will*
> *help you gain more control of the outcome.*

Many recommend using the "carrot and the stick" approach in many projects. My personal experience with hundreds of projects over many years is that getting others to become *evangelical* and excited about the project is the most effective way. Management by intimidation can work for short periods of time, but even the least democratic of management institutions—an army—understands that teamwork, communications, mission, and training all create better outcomes for projects with a lot of risk in them. If your team members believe that it's possible, they transfer that excitement and message to their staff and partners.

While most don't want to talk about it, penalties are written into contracts and projects for a reason. They are the safety net to ensure that the "best-case effort" is made to get the work done on time and on budget. In the case where that does not happen, then some level of that risk is offset by a penalty.

Penalties, in the most common format, are self-inflicted wounds. Bidding a project on a fixed-price, fixed-time-frame basis is dangerous if those delivering the project do not to stay within the project milestones. The original owner of the project may get a good deal on price but will likely suffer because of delayed deadlines.

## VISUALIZING YOUR PROJECT

One of the most complex issues about larger-scale project management is visualizing what is happening. If someone in an organization asks the status of a project and cannot get it, it means there is a problem, a communication problem.

For many years, consultants, project managers, and software developers have focused on the issue of seeing what is happening in a project. It is hard to understand the status of a project without a visual cue. Visualization is the answer—seeing what the status is, what is supposed to happen next, who is going to do it, and how much it will cost. All of these factors are often wrapped up in complex software products that need specialists to see what is going on inside them. Are we there yet? Simple questions deserve simple and accurate answers. Communicating what is going on also means that you have to understand what is happening from your perspective. The answer is to visualize the project status.

If others can visualize the plan and *understand* that visual image, then communication has been successful. Visualize your plan; if you can see it, you can improve it. So ensure that the diagrams used provide the detail you want. Table 5.2 contains some examples.

As you can see, some of these results are inscrutable. In general, simple is better, and while there was more work in creating the PowerPoint file, using links, project status, and updates provide desirable features at a low cost.

TABLE 5.2 *Milestones, Time Frames, and Time Lines*

| TASK | ROLES | RESOURCES | TIME | GUIDELINES | MILESTONE |
|---|---|---|---|---|---|
| Determine proposal type | Inside sales rep | | 12 min | Sales manual | Proposal type determined |
| Select proposal template | Sales admin | Template library | 12 min | | Proposal template selected |
| Populate template | Sales admin | CRM | 12 min | | Template populated |
| Customize boilerplate text | Sales rep | MS Word | 60 min | Sales manual | Text customized |
| Write new proposal text | Sales rep | MS Word | 30 min | Sales manual | Text written |
| Determine pricing | Sales rep | | 30 min | Price book | Pricing determined |
| Approve pricing | Sales mgr | | 15 min | Price book | Pricing approved |
| Determine if override required | Sales admin | | 10 min | Price book | Override needed |
| Approve pricing override | VP Sales | | 20 min | Price book, Sales manual | Override approved |
| Finalize proposal document | Sales rep | | 60 min | | Proposal finalized |
| Send proposal | Sales admin | FedEx, e-mail | 10 min | | Proposal sent |

The swim lane model in Figure 5.10 is good for showing the roles of those involved, but it is missing a lot of detail. Any changes mean the whole drawing has to be changed manually—lots of work. TaskMap (Figure 5.11) represents a middle ground between the project management system generated, a Gantt chart (Figure 5.12), and a process map. Details are there and understandable, but some specialized software investment is required for the Visio and TaskMap systems.

Bottom line: Investing in the labor effort to create a visual view of your project increases the ability of others to understand deadlines, dependencies, and its progress to date. The amount of the investment is dependent on your resources and budget.

Now that we have the project under way, we have to turn ourselves to the last step of keeping our project on time and on budget: managing the project.

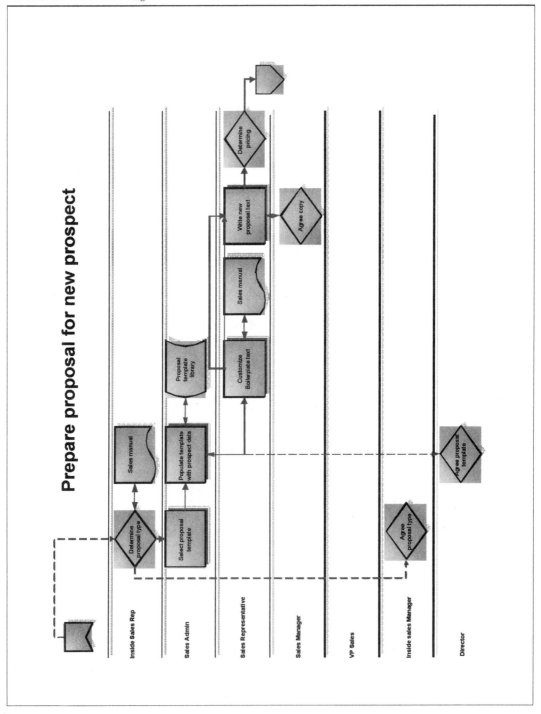

FIGURE 5.10  *Swim Lane Diagram*

FIGURE 5.11 *TaskMap® Example*

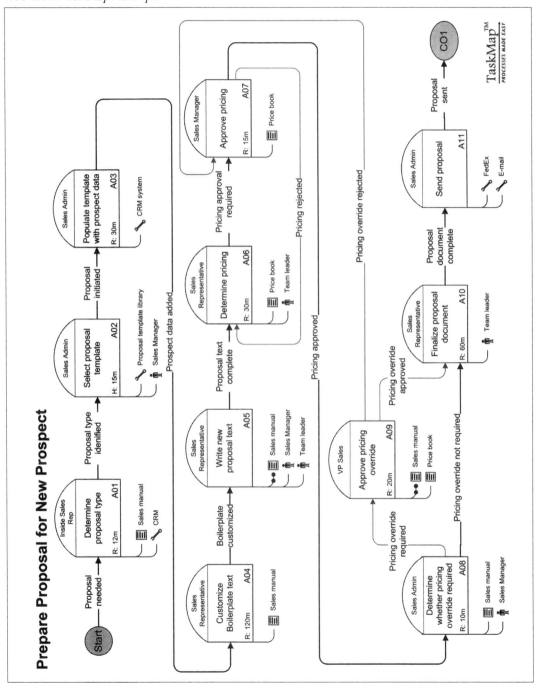

FIGURE 5.12 *Gantt Chart*

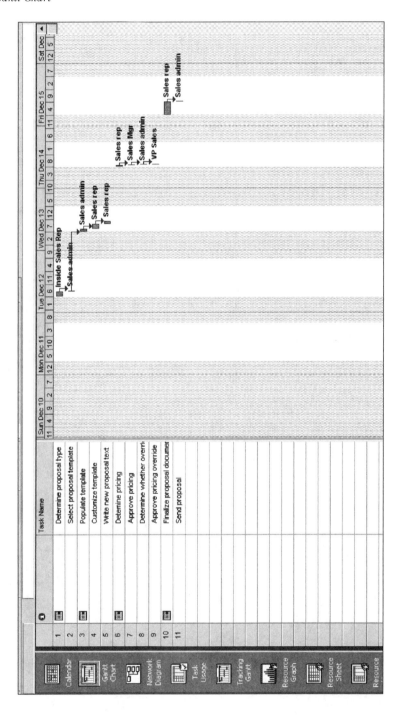

# 6

# STEP 3: MANAGE

*"Good thoughts are no better than good dreams, unless they be executed."*
**Ralph Waldo Emerson**

**N**ow that the project is under way, we reach that most critical of all steps, ensuring that it is successful—*managing*. There are many aspects to this phase: keeping it on time and on budget, making sure it meets the goals, and watching other external factors that may impact its success, among others. There's a lot to do, and now—with much riding on success—we are right in the middle of it. The project's train has left the station, and we have to keep it moving in the right direction.

## CONTROLLING YOUR PROJECT

The first factor in any project management scenario is the issue of control. In project management this word is used in two ways. *Control (v)*–exercising restraint and directing influence over the project, and *control (n)*–a tool, instrument, technique, or artistic medium to help you maintain your authority over the project.

Controlling tasks and their successful completion is the foundation for effective projects and outcomes.

> Control yourself: *Control (v)*—exercising restraint and directing influence over the project. *Control (n)*—a tool, instrument, technique, or artistic medium to help you maintain your authority over the project.

Setting up controls should be a part of the project plan and should have a great deal of transparency. Controls set levels in place for quality, materials, cost estimates versus actual costs, time frame, and standards; each should be clear to those involved. It is your role as project manager to construct this framework for management and control.

Understanding how these elements relate and affect each other is one important aspect of control. When you lose control of one element, it has an impact on another. Therefore, the dependencies within the project management process require viewing as a complete entity. These are a living, breathing mass of variables that need to be contained and proactively managed.

## Management Style

The management style taken on a project has more bearing on success than might be first thought. The many jokes about the various stages of a project from *punishing the innocent* to *rewarding the undeserving* all have some truth hidden in the humor.

There are always cases in life where the individuals responsible do not always get their just desserts. In the long run, however, those with good morals, a work ethic, and fair management approaches will prevail. While team members may emerge unscathed from a difficult project, they are more willing to work with those who treated them and others fairly. Beware of project managers who talk only about protecting their team and "screwing" the other partners in the process. You can imagine what will be said about you once you are on the other side.

Business ethics are becoming an important issue for managers today. Unfortunately, the fact that we even have to train managers that being honest and fair is a requirement is amazing—as if lying and cheating were the normal behavior taught in business school and the workplace. Treat others as you would like to be treated, and results will pour out from unexpected quarters. Team members will rise to the occasion because they want the project to be successful for them, the team, and for you, their project leader.

Our individual management style is something that emerges and changes over time. Every experience enhances our knowledge, both good and bad. Considering each project a learning event is a good way to look at it. However, do not take reaching goals and objectives lightly. As an assigned project manager, you will get the credit—or the blame—depending on the results.

Reducing risk by using best practices is one way to supplement learning the hard way; that comes through experience alone. The following areas highlight some of those areas where a project needs controlling. As mentioned during the last chapter, ensure that you have an up-to-date picture of the status of the project available to you at all times. That way you can keep a pulse on things before they get out of control.

## Costs

During the estimating/planning phase of the project, cost is one element that affects many others. Because costs have many characteristics and variables, it is important to ensure they are clearly understood before adding cost controls into the project.

Assuming the picture you paint in the planning stage is accurate as the project moves along, you must still keep a close eye on cost elements and how they affect the results of each milestone or activity.

Some variables on cost that need to be tracked include:

- Fixed costs (labor and materials)
- Variable costs (labor and materials)
- Time-sensitive costs (weather conditions, delivery, other dependencies)
- Unexpected costs and variables

Wherever possible, highlight the ones moving out of control and ensure suppliers and vendors maintain "not-to-exceed" limits. That is even more important if this is the first project experience with a particular supplier. Payment schedules are important to adhere to, especially if a payment is dependent on reaching a milestone.

## Time Frames

Another fundamental element in maintaining control of a project is managing time frames. While cost is one part of the time frame equation, there are others. These include:

- Meeting the deadline
- Staying on time within the budget
- Watching time dependencies

The most obvious time frame to manage is the deadline. Deadlines can be created to coincide with a milestone or deliverable. While this may seem a good practice, it does in fact cause some problems. This is because the deadline is at the end of the milestone, so it is not often reviewed until that milestone is almost due or has passed. This is usually too late.

Time frames have to be dissected into manageable pieces to be controlled. For example, a certain milestone is the delivery of the specification document on a certain date. In order for this to be completed there is a variety of tasks in the process of building the specification document. Research, first drafts, reviews, and any approval cycles are all necessary. By looking at each part of this process—a series of tasks, or miniprocesses—it is easier to spot where problems are occurring before they get out of hand. In this case, waiting until the last week before the deadline hits does not allow time for changes to occur.

By looking at the project as separate, timed elements leading up to deadlines and milestones, it becomes much easier to stay in control. Over time, you gain almost a sixth sense for the ones that will likely cause the most trouble. By identifying where inexperienced staff or insufficient resources may cause delays, you can then factor in extra time to effect a recovery operation.

FIGURE 6.1 *Control Points*

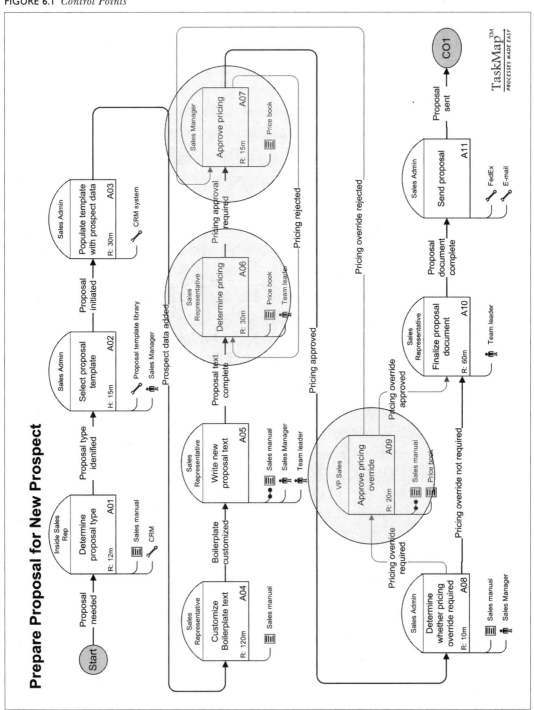

Another big problem with staying on time is the budget issue. The old "time is money" maxim is unfortunately true. The effect on budget can be huge when milestones or deadlines dependent on each other are missed. All the resources have been allocated to start programming work on a project but the design team is a month behind. When projects are people dependent, resources are often scheduled weeks and months in advance. Development teams that have to work on tight deadlines—such as race teams preparing for an upcoming season—understand the importance of interdependent deadlines.

Vehicle manufacturers competing in race series must have production bikes and cars in place by a certain date, because lining up sponsors, mechanics, and drivers takes time. If they miss the date for entry, they wait till next season. Poor planning and missed deadlines in execution can make a huge difference to marketing plans and financial performance in the ensuing year. The manufacturers have to stay on track (excuse the pun) and meet the deadline with a product meeting stringent requirements.

As the previous example makes clear, another element with time worth flagging is the deadline with dependencies. Rather like a family with children, there is just more to worry about. Keeping them healthy, getting them off to school, and feeding and clothing them makes them dependent on you as parents. The same applies to your project; it has deadlines and milestones that are also dependent and therefore require managing more carefully. The more points there are where the project can run off the rails, the greater the number and complexity of dependencies.

The sum of the parts is greater than the whole is a well-known phrase. In the case of managing time in a project, it can be the reverse. It may be better to change the scope of items in a project if you run the risk of missing a critical deadline. This trade-off is made all the time in many projects, such as home building, software development, and restoration projects.

*Deadlines Gone Wild!* One of the funniest examples of deadlines gone wild is the Tom Hanks movie *The Money Pit.* It clearly indicates that anything that is dependent on something else can and will go wrong at times in a project. Unlike many projects in the real world, Hanks found he was unable to compromise on either quality or time frame, thus running the budget out of sight. The movie made for amusing viewing, but unfortunately many real-world examples are less entertaining.

> *It may be better to change the scope of items
> in a project if you run the risk of missing
> a critical deadline.*

## Quality

Standards of quality and quality control remain a difficult item for many to quantify when controlling a project. Some questions have to be answered, and hopefully will have been integrated into the plan.

- How much quality can I afford?
- What is the impact of low quality?
- Can I communicate these quality standards and requirements to my suppliers and vendors?

These standards may already be well defined, and control points added into the project. Unfortunately, there is always some subjectivity to quality standards, and often others do not understand them well. For example, the difference in how much effort should be expended in matters of style in Italy versus other parts of the world may be difficult to comprehend. Style has a huge impact on almost all aspects of products or services in Italy; from the restaurants, clothes, automobiles, and housing—how something looks is part of its form and function. In Italy, quality means form and function.

Because quality standards can vary, it is vital to you, as a project manager, that participants in the project know what is required and have the budget, resources, and guidelines to ensure that it's going to meet your standards. While industrial standards provide one metric to consider, they are usually too broad for decision making and management in a specific project.

As an example, the aerospace industry has its standards and guidelines set by the Air Transport Association (ATA) regarding maintenance procedures and requirements. Does that mean that all quality standards by manufacturers meet only those standards? Of course not. Each vendor or airline sets its own bar for quality standards, and the ATA standards become the lowest common denominator. Quality within a project needs to meet the requirements and expectations of the goals and objectives. The quality standard applied to an external outbuilding or garage might be very different from those of a heated and cooled living area added to the house or apartment.

Control points for quality should have specific guidelines, agreed and understood in advance of the project start. In addition, other certification or professional standards may also be required for vendors and suppliers. It may be a requirement that suppliers in engineering fields have ISO9002 or ISO14000 certification. This ensures that some level of competency has been shown in reaching these standards.

For project milestones, guidelines that incorporate satisfactory standards that need following should be made clear. Sometimes this is obvious and at other times less so. For example, wood sap seeping through fresh paint on a new house might indicate that it was not sealed or primed properly, and a visual-quality check makes it clear the subcontractor has some extra work to clear it up. However, other areas such as the quality of insulation materials or the types of nails used in external woodwork may never come to light. The only way to ensure that these are being done to your standards is to agree on them up front and then have a monitoring means to check this was the material standard requested or method of construction used.

Projects involving software development have an even wider berth in terms of quality. Sometimes the same result in terms of code and functionality can be created using less memory and resources because of the method of architecture and initial design. Unfortunately, because it is often easy to continue making modifications to design and requirements, some systems build on less-than-perfect foundations and only find their way to the market by way of extensive testing and quality-assurance fixes.

Inserting quality checkpoints along the way in your project plan is one way to keep these issues in check and under control.

*Because quality standards can vary,*
*it is vital that you, as a project manager,*
*are sure that participants in the project*
*know what is required and have the budget,*
*resources, and guidelines to ensure*
*that it's going to meet your standards.*

## Other Standards

It is often quipped that the nice thing about standards is that there are so many to choose from; while a little overused, it is also true. In the same way, different individuals and groups view quality standards differently, which can really hurt a project.

Nowhere is that more true than in the world of independent contractors. Whether offering building services or becoming an expert consultant, many offer little in the way of achieved standards or qualifications to justify the newfound shingle on their door.

This also applies to general contractors, who are often no more than inexperienced middlemen providing a stream of work to others and providing no oversight or added value. It is amazing how one person's skills in an unrelated area appear to qualify that person for some other subject matter he or she knows nothing about. As you can probably tell, reading between the lines, there is some personal hurt here. My experience can be used to your benefit. Check the references, verify insurance and licenses, and try to do the project on a fixed price if you can.

Other standards that are important from the project perspective also can be categorized as guidelines. These can be operating procedures, controls, instructions, standards, safety procedures, tips, recipes, formulae, and more that require following. In some cases, the standards followed for the project deliverables are part of the milestones. As an example, a supplier provides an engine as part of an engineering project; to support that engine, guidelines are needed for installation, maintenance, and support activities. Certain required standards should be within the documentation for the project along with control points for standards to be met.

FIGURE 6.2 *Guidelines and the Control Factors That Influence Their Effectiveness*

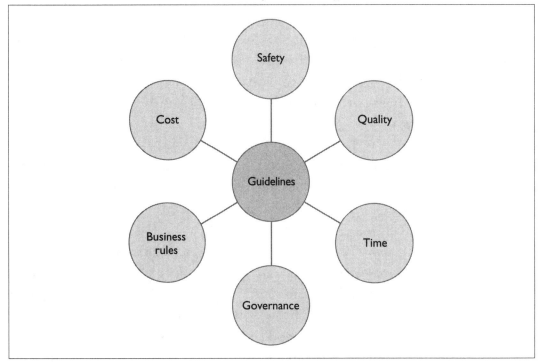

## MANAGEMENT APPROACHES AND TOOLS

In addition to our control points to identify areas of concern and keep them under control, it is also essential to use the very best possible management approaches and tools.

After the project is under way, managing the product schedule is the first place to begin. The creation of an effective management schedule for the project can be as important as monitoring performance.

Tasks involved in managing the project are different from those involved in the creation and delivery of the project results. In general they are broken into five categories:

1. Monitoring and assessing progress

2. Communication of the project's progress

3. Assessing the need for change

4. Facilitation, documenting, and agreeing to the change

5. Modifying the schedule/project plan to accommodate the change

Each of these has its own particular set of tasks and, as Figure 6.3 illustrates, order of execution. There is not, however, a notation on how to deal with the management of each task.

Figure 6.4 illustrates application of the tasks listed.

If all is going well with a project, the control points scheduled are on track, and quality and milestones are being met, then only tasks 1 and 2 will be required. When things start going awry, the need for real project management skills kicks in. The other three categories will need serious application to bring things back under control.

FIGURE 6.3 *Project Management Schedule*

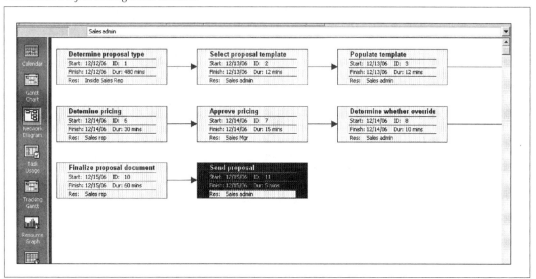

FIGURE 6.4 *Managing Projects*

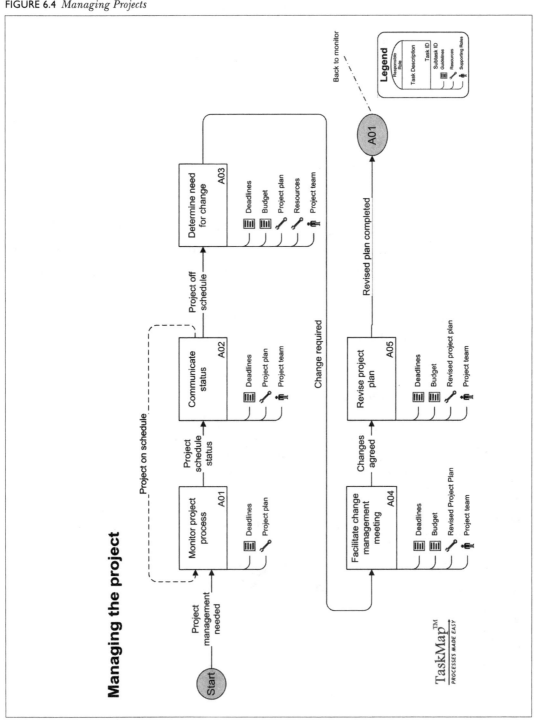

## Monitoring and Assessing the Project's Progress

Setting up a management schedule for a regular review and reporting method is the first stage of monitoring and assessment. Achieve this by capturing the relevant control points from the project, quality, deadlines, deliverables, standards, and so on and then determining if the project is on schedule and sharing the relevant information with the team.

The task order here is *capture* the project status, *monitor* its progress, and *assess* the status. If all is well, then report as such. Providing the team with reporting requirements in advance of meetings so members can review project status greatly improves the efficiency of this process.

## Communicating the Project's Progress

Communications of a project's progress should have several topics covered in as much or as little detail as is relevant for the team. These would include:

- Milestones, tasks, and deadlines *completed*
- Milestones, tasks, and deadlines in progress and *on schedule*
- Milestones, tasks, and deadlines in progress but *at risk*
- Milestones, tasks, and deadlines *missed*

If all is going well, the first two categories may be all you need communicate at status meetings; but if some are at risk, additional actions need to be taken.

**FIGURE 6.5** *Monitoring Project Tasks and Their Relationships*

| | | Task Name | Duration | Start |
|---|---|---|---|---|
| | 1 | Determine proposal type | 480 mins | Tue 12/12/06 |
| | 2 | Select proposal template | 12 mins | Wed 12/13/06 |
| | 3 | Populate template | 12 mins | Wed 12/13/06 |
| | 4 | Customize template | 120 mins | Thu 12/14/06 |
| | 5 | Write new proposal text | 576 mins | Thu 12/14/06 |
| | 6 | Determine pricing | 30 mins | Thu 12/14/06 |
| | 7 | Approve pricing | 15 mins | Thu 12/14/06 |
| | 8 | Determine whether overric | 10 mins | Thu 12/14/06 |
| | 9 | Approve pricing override | 20 mins | Thu 12/14/06 |
| | 10 | Finalize proposal documen | 60 mins | Fri 12/15/06 |
| | 11 | Send proposal | 5 mins | Fri 12/15/06 |

# Accessing the Need for Change

> *. . . as problems arise, take a deep breath,*
> *look at the alternatives, and move forward.*

Once this occurs, our skill at identifying problems and how to deal with them comes to the forefront. The first stage is to assess the severity of the problem. If we find that the severity is not too bad, then perhaps additional resources, a scope change, or some staff increase may resolve the issue. In the same way that we have assessed risk in other parts of the project definition and management process, it is good to assign some level of risk to the issue.

This has the advantage of determining the actions to be taken, which can be particularly important if there are several areas being assessed at the same time. A more common factor is parallel activities all heading toward the same deadline or milestone. These need special recognition to determine when the need to change occurs.

Some outcomes from the assessment process may include the following:

1. No change required
2. Need to reduce the scope to stay on time
3. Increase resources
4. Modify approach and design to get back on schedule
5. Let the schedule slip here and pick up later
6. Cancel the project
7. Change the milestone and deadline

While this book has "on time and on budget" in the subtitle, there will be times when the project time line or budget just has to change. By looking at the project in its entirety, making the tradeoffs listed above can be managed and the right combination picked for the circumstances.

It is amazing that a frequent reaction to project problems is to start out with a liberal dose of blame and fireworks, as if that helps to solve the problem. While this may have some cathartic benefits for the admonisher, it will do little for the team. So as problems arise, take a deep breath, look at the alternatives, and move forward.

As these management challenges arise, tackling them in a logical and calm manner also creates the appropriate problem-solving attitude in the rest of the team. Radical action such as canceling the project is usually taken only in dire circumstances, but it is an option that is sometimes better than the alternative if the project is so far off track that it cannot possibly meet the goals initially set.

*It is amazing that a frequent reaction
to project problems is to start out with a
liberal dose of blame and fireworks, as if
that helps to solve the problem. While this
may have some cathartic benefits for the
admonisher, it will do little for the team.*

An information technology example at the U.S. Internal Revenue Service illustrates that millions of dollars can be wasted on a project if it is not managed well, but at least someone had the guts in the end to cancel the project and not waste more.

## Facilitating the Change

Once you make an assessment, the next stage is to determine what actions to take. As project manager, you will likely have this responsibility and will be required to produce results.

*Facilitation is often a place where logical rules
meet soft skills.*

Facilitation is often a place where logical rules meet soft skills. Logical rules help in ensuring that facilitating change follows good business practices and the soft skills are getting the best out of the project team.

As Figure 6.6 illustrates, taking logical steps to determine actions and gaining agreement for change is important; once agreed, an often missed step is to document them. The number of times I have heard the mantra "I don't recall agreeing to that!" is significant. In the excitement of gaining the agreement, project managers forget to document things.

FIGURE 6.6 *Logical Steps for First Stages of Facilitating and Documenting Change*

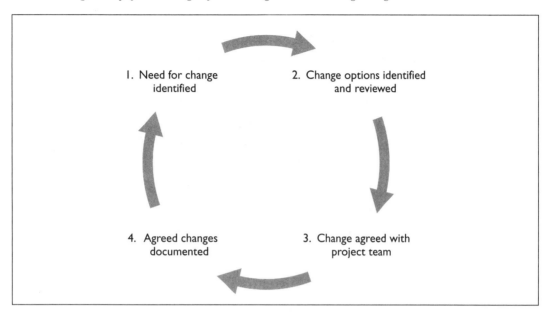

As each modification to the plan is obviously a change, then some form of change control has to be a part of the project management process. In these past few pages we have been walking through the basic elements of change control, assessing risks, determining actions, and agreement of changes, and now we have to modify the project plan.

## Updating the Plan

Any time there is a need for change and an agreement regarding what action to take, transfer it to the project plan. Every time a change is made, a new version should be created with a notation of what has changed and why.

If these changes affect other team members' schedules, it is even more important to notify those members at the earliest possible stage. Remember, it is the project manager's responsibility to keep an eye on all the moving parts of the project. If possible, provide a visual update to the plan, including changes in resources, guidelines, staffing levels, deadlines, and milestones. If a visual plan was created in the first place, it will be easier to update it on a regular basis. Even an e-mail summary can be a good way of notifying the team in a simple and efficient manner of what changes have occurred and why.

Do not underestimate the need to overcommunicate. In the same way that a real estate agent uses the mantra Location, Location, Location, in project management the same has to be said of communication. Keeping the team informed of good news as well as bad helps everyone through difficult times that inevitably occur.

As a wrap-up to managing the project effectively, return to a topic touched on in the planning section. Saved for last here, it is central to not just initial goal setting but to keeping the project real. If the team thinks the project goals are not achievable at the start, the potential to achieve results is severely impaired.

## SETTING EXPECTATIONS

Many will tell you that setting expectations is one of the most important aspects of success in managing projects. While this may be true, it is also true that setting the goalposts low to ensure you can kick the ball through does not mean that others will be impressed. Setting goals and then meeting them are certainly important, but meeting mediocre goals that do not impress others will not likely win anything in the long run.

FIGURE 6.7 *Updated Plan*

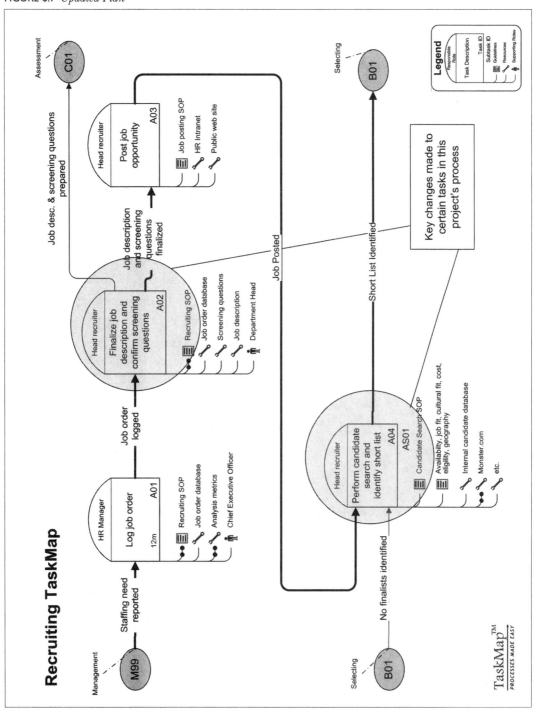

Similarly, setting meteoric goals that will never be achieved also might cause others to consider your project plan and goals unattainable. While many leaders will point out that you achieve nothing worthwhile without setting very high goals, in project management you need to get others to buy in. Tough goals yes, unreachable goals no.

*Tough goals yes, unreachable goals no.*

If you are a first-time project manager and just setting out in the world, you have one huge advantage over experienced managers—you don't know what you can't do. During my early 20s, a few years ago I will admit now, I continued to receive projects and assignments that seemed way beyond my capabilities and experience. For some reason, I just managed to make it through the learning experience and out to the other side. Part determination, part stubbornness, the results always seemed to come.

*"You do not lead by hitting people over the head—*
*that's assault, not leadership . . ."*

Dwight D. Eisenhower

In retrospect, some of those assignments today would not be easy for me to achieve. Why? Because knowing what I know now, the risk level for success would be outside a comfort and knowledge zone that makes up my character and persona today. As a young and inexperienced individual, I didn't know I couldn't do it. My manager set the goals and left the rest to me. Sink or swim. Live or die. The results were the goals. The method and project plan were up to me to figure out.

So experience can be a handicap as well as a friend. If I had had the experience so I could have avoided those early pitfalls, then I could have achieved even more at that young age.

Understanding the balance between being able to do something individually with huge effort and intellect and needing a team around you to meet those same lofty goals will help you control the outcomes of your projects much more effectively.

*Experience can be a handicap as well as a friend. If you are a first-time project manager just setting out in the world, you have one huge advantage over experienced managers– you don't know what you can't do.*

A major factor in setting expectations is separating your individual ability to do something from the rest of the project team. It's worth rereading that last sentence . . . separating your *individual ability* from the rest of the project team. Your team may consist of just you and a coworker, partner, or spouse. Even so, you have to get them bought in if you are going to have them share in the results.

Part of this is doing what is called dividing the work. There are usually two roles for every project manager: (1) your part doing work in the project and (2) managing the project.

This simple concept is very important at the expectation-setting stage of a project. If you are running the project but also have to participate by actually doing real work in it, then the first place to start is to understand what you can and cannot do.

It is better to focus on the management aspect of the project if you cannot invest the time or energy to bring your expertise up to do your part of the job. A simple example was some remodeling at home with my wife. It started out with a single bathroom, where we researched the techniques and materials to get the job done, did the design, and got to it. In this case my wife (who is an excellent do-it-yourselfer) was the project manager, but it was important that the workers help-ing her (my son and I) provided the labor and materials as needed during the program.

If you are going to operate as a general contractor for a home-building project, you better have some idea of how you are going to schedule materials, tradesmen, and laborers along with the planning process. In some cases you may find yourself as a project manager only; in others you are responsi-ble for actually getting the work done.

## ORDER IN THE HOUSE

In the change management section of this chapter we dis-cussed the order of tasks and milestones. As your project man-agement experience increases, it becomes ever more obvious that the order of project milestones and their management is changeable.

A super way to cut down the time frames and meet dead-lines in projects with a very deliberate and sequential sched-ule is to change the order of events. This is often done with parallel processes, effectively starting up several aspects of the project to run concurrently rather than in sequence. In-stead of waiting for milestone one, two, and three to be achieved over time, they can be started in parallel with addi-tional resources to meet the impending deadlines.

Almost every business today and, in particular, almost ev-ery supply chain project anywhere on the planet use the prin-ciple of concurrent processes. Once learned, you will begin to look for ways to reduce risk, compress time frames, and opti-mize results using parallel processes or changing the order of tasks and activities in your project plan.

FIGURE 6.8 *Concurrent Processes*

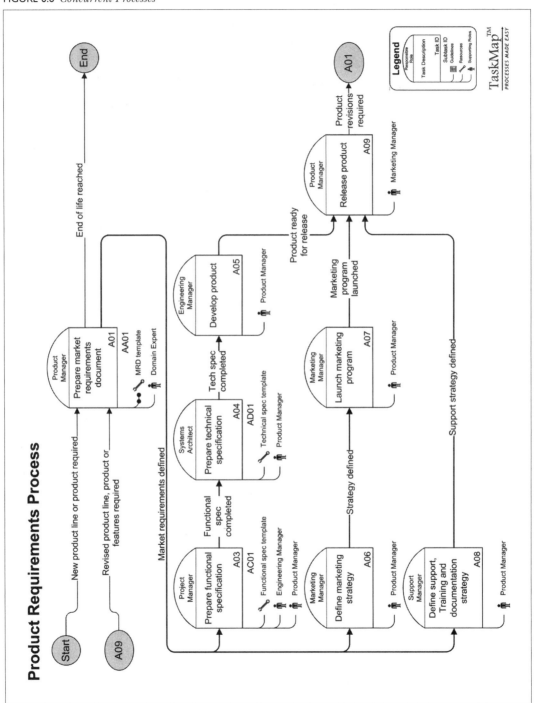

Advanced techniques such as paralleling processes and running concurrent activities will increase as your project management skills improve.

A great deal of the practices in this section come with years of combined experiences, some earned very much the hard way. As you move on to managing your own projects, individual learning experiences will continue to hone your own skills. Even from the difficult experiences that may lie ahead in some projects, absorb the good and the bad from them, and then ensure that you avoid the same mistakes the next time out.

# 7

# SAMPLE PROJECTS

**T**his chapter illustrates the development, implementation, and management of two projects—one simple and one complex—and the decision-making processes associated with each one. As you read this chapter, it should become clear to you that both simple and complex projects use the no-nonsense project management vocabulary combined with the three-step project management process.

However, risk factors, changes, and managing expectations had a significant impact on the projects' success and the results achieved. The first project is a do-it-yourself (D-I-Y) project—removing and replacing a toilet—a task that many of us can tackle given a few tools and basic plumbing skills.

# PROJECT ONE—REPAIRING AND REPLACING A TOILET

This project represents a fairly simple plumbing problem, one that has faced many; but like many other "simple" projects, things can go wrong if not executed correctly.

For the purposes of this project, make the assumption that we are not plumbers and therefore do not have the required subject matter expertise to do this job in our sleep. At the outset of the project, we look at the goals and objectives.

## Goals and Objectives

1. Replace the current old commode with a modern unit.
2. Cost of the replacement unit should not exceed $150.
3. Total cost allocated for the project is $250 including materials.
4. Project should take no longer than two days to complete.

These goals and objectives create some significant input to the planning phase of the project. With local plumbers costing as much as $75 per hour and estimates of two to three hours to complete the work, the project is definitely in the do-it-yourself category; otherwise it will be impossible to stay within the budget and time frame.

## Planning

During this step, we need to determine what is going to be required for the job. In this case we would also do some research, as we are unfamiliar with the tasks involved and the best way to manage them.

We can become educated about this topic in several ways:

- Take a trip to the hardware store and request help from its staff regarding the best way to tackle the project.
- Do some online research to look for instructions on how best to remove and replace the toilet.
- Purchase a book on D-I-Y plumbing that covers the topic.

Many D-I-Y projects have very poor planning characteristics, often because they are projects that we have been procrastinating about and the SO (significant other) has pushed us directly into action. This action often means pressing on to "visible" activity and often bypassing the planning process. In this case, as with many home projects, when we are not really sure how to do it, but "how hard could it be" is at the forefront, many things end up going wrong. This usually results in multiple trips to the hardware store, purchasing tools that we may use only once, continued frustration about missing something, and finally breakages. This material often creates enough copy for a comedy show but does little for relationships, particularly as the project usually occurs over precious free time.

The point here is that some basic research will avoid many of these problems and allow you to create a list of tools, materials, and instructions that will help you avoid many of the above issues. During the research phase we are able to procure information about the removal process, what tools will be required, the tasks to be taken, and the order in which to do them, as well as some basic information on cost.

So gradually our project plan is coming together, and we can start to estimate costs to ensure that we can stay within our budget guidelines.

- *Resources*—Replacement toilet, seals, fittings, plumbers' wrench
- *People and roles*—Do-it-yourselfer
- *Time*—Weekend
- *Cost*—Toilet $100, seals and fittings $20, wrench $20; total estimate $140
- *Guidelines*—Step-by-step guide for removal and replacement of toilet

So our five elements are identified and we now need to have some sort of plan to ensure that this goes swimmingly when it comes to implementation.

Our big risk is probably not the cost element, although there may be tools or materials needed that we have overlooked. The big risk is our inexperience and ensuring that excellent step-by-step instructions are there so we do not make a big mess of something as a result of our inexperience and lack of knowledge here.

Some research on the Internet provides a lot of written guidelines, but it is still not really clear what has to happen.

## Implementation

The following two diagrams (Figures 7.1 and 7.2) illustrate the value of using instructions to provide a step-by-step guide to what is required for each task in the project. In this case a picture is worth a thousand words, and in fact the two diagrams replace about 1,200 words with a process map illustrating each task in the project.

FIGURE 7.1  *Removal Instructions in TaskMap® Format*

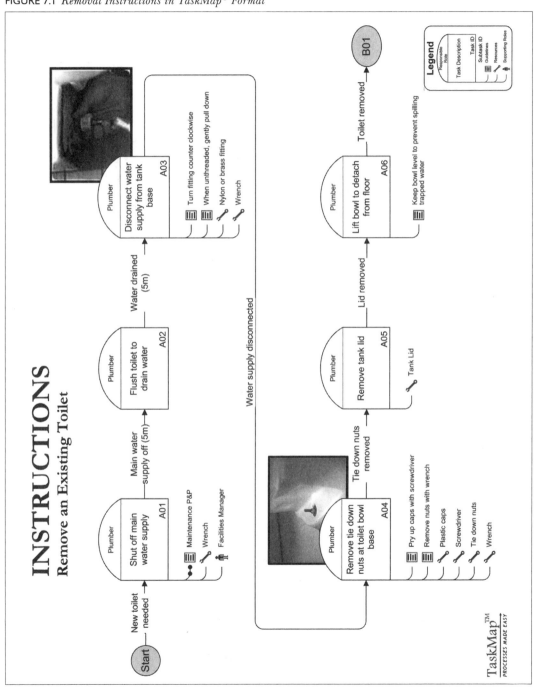

Courtesy Harvard Computing Group

FIGURE 7.2 *Installation Instructions in TaskMap® Format*

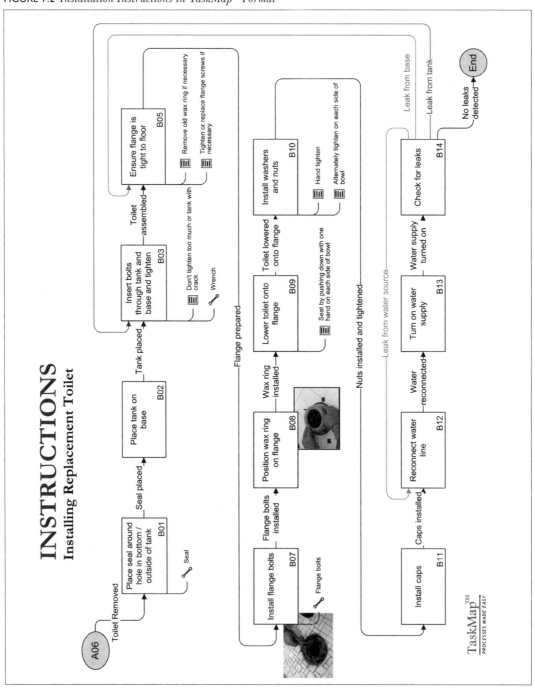

Courtesy Harvard Computing Group

In the model a task box represents the tasks, along with guidelines for each task. In this case the guidelines are actual instructions for the task at hand. Additional information regarding the resources required has a wrench next to it, and a legend in the bottom corner of the page makes it easy for readers to follow the plan.

This type of visualization aid not just helps you understand the tasks in your project but what the outcomes should be from each step. As this project is something that can be done in a matter of hours, the milestones are likely to be

1. complete planning phase;

2. complete toilet removal; and

3. complete toilet replacement.

The level of detail is high because of the person doing the job's lack of subject matter knowledge. More detail and instruction are needed to complement the worker's skill level or, in this case, lack of it. If the plumber had been hired for the project, instructions would not have been needed, just materials for the job.

Once the second milestone has been reached, the next stage in the project occurs: replacing the toilet. By following the instructions in Figure 7.2, it becomes clear what tasks and guidelines require following. Note in this case that added pictorial instructions further improve the clarity of the project plan.

In cases such as this, pictorial instructions reduce risk and makes it easier for the person following the plan. The person can identify the area requiring work, follow the task, and see what the result should be.

The acquisition of the materials and tools was through a local hardware warehouse store. As most of these have a liberal return policy, unused additional items are easily returnable.

Another good practice: make sure you have enough material for the job. In this case, for example, it's pretty easy to mess up the seal if you do not set it down correctly, so having a "spare" doesn't hurt.

## Project Management

In this example, aside from making sure that you have enough help to lift the fixtures, there is not a lot of project management involved. Be careful not to drop porcelain (it doesn't bounce well), follow the tasks in order, and, most important, make sure that the water is off before you start.

In the case of your own time, it is likely you will take much longer than a professional plumber will, but as you are not being paid, this probably doesn't matter as much. Unless, of course, you can earn more than the plumber can, you might want to consider hiring one while spending your time doing something more valuable.

As noted in the replacement diagram, monitoring certain items for leaks after reconnection is very important to check. By using a visual representation of the project tasks and their order, it is simple to provide guidance when things go wrong.

# PROJECT TWO—COMPLEX RESEARCH AND RECOMMENDATIONS PROJECT

At the other end of the spectrum we examine a project that has some of the most difficult variables imaginable in a project. In 2003, USAID (United States Agency for International Development) submitted a bid for a market research project to assist with the development of the Information and Communications Technology sector in Egypt. The goal of this project was to determine what actions would improve skills, marketing, and sales activities for the development of an entire industry sector. It goes without saying that this was quite a handful. This project also had further complications associated with the initial planning stage, including the following:

- The project would involve interviewing more than 160 organizations.
- Other countries with similar development challenges should be benchmarked.
- All of the interviews for the Egyptian portion had to be done on-site.
- Work had to be coordinated between several AID groups, industry sectors, and education and government on the ground in Egypt.
- The project was to have a fixed price with fixed deadlines for delivery over a nine-month period.
- All deliverables would be reviewed and approved prior to final payments.

And this was just the requirement for the proposal work.

## Planning

Right from the start, this project had the ingredients for some significant problems in terms of goal definition; and there were four customers and two separate deliverables, as it turned out. In this situation one of the most important elements was ensuring that the planning was right on the money. With a requirement for the Egyptian government, USAID, and two huge U.S. contracting firms involved, the margin for error was zero.

In situations like this where a large project looms but there are different uses for the resulting materials, it is often better to take baby steps first before putting it all out there and risking deliverables.

The planning stage for this project actually consisted of creating a plan for the plan. Let me explain. Because the parties involved wanted to ensure that each group bought into the program and we were going to take differing actions from the output of the study, it was crucial everyone agreed on the methodology of the plan as well as the detail level of the results.

Consequently, the first stage of the project was to visit Egypt and the first contractor on the project and work with their team to create a plan for the plan.

## Preplanning Research

Given the complexity of doing research in another country as well as a number of variables in the deliverables, it became necessary to create a framework for what was to be delivered to the client as well as to gain agreement with all the various parties that the approach was going to work well. In this case there were several challenging issues, including these:

- Ensure that the data collected would be accurate, but also maintain the confidentiality of the participants.

- Gain the agreement from all parties that the proposed methodology would be culturally acceptable to them.

- Avoid overlap with other projects in the country and share data among AID groups.

The first month of the project consisted of building a framework outlined in the following section. This ended up being the basis of the large project plan in the months that followed.

## Objectives and Goals

The following pages represent the basis of the project plan. Here the prospective client has a clear set of goals, objectives, milestones, and deliverables associated with the project.

- To conduct and deliver an Information and Communication Technology (ICT) Skills Gap Analysis

- Sector Assessment of the Egyptian ICT including direct comparisons to other countries that have successfully developed industry infrastructures and export programs

The goals were to define the size and profile of the Egyptian ICT sector in all its segments and for other selected sectors, clusters, and firms, including the number and types of organizations, dollar value, and comparison to other international competitive markets, including Ireland, Israel, India, and Jordan.

- To evaluate and identify the capabilities, strengths, and weaknesses of the Egyptian ICT industry, specifically to perform a Skills Gap Analysis for the supply component of the industry

This sector assessment consisted of an evaluation of 35 to 45 organizations designated to be part of this project. Senior software industry consultants from Harvard Computing Group (HCG) visited each of these groups. During these visits they evaluated each organization's technology, staff skills, methodology, and potential competitiveness in both local and international markets. Educational and service organizations were also included in this study.

Harvard Computing Group prepared a final sector assessment report and analysis that described the various industry

TABLE 7.1 *Stages and Time Line*

| PROJECT PHASE | ESTIMATED COMPLETION DATE | DELIVERABLE |
|---|---|---|
| Phase One—Background research on competitive markets | February 2003 | Background materials for the report and visit to Egypt to collect data for study |
| Phase Two—Research on Egyptian market (to be conducted in Egypt) | March 2003 | |
| Phase Three—Research of target organizations | March 2003 | Input to the report |
| Phase Four—Report development and delivery | August 2003 | Report and recommendations |

strengths and challenges, and provided recommended future steps. It also provided liaison support to the rest of the teams to ensure that there was commonality and the transfer of research instruments, strategy, and output for other projects associated with this study.

## Tasks, Processes, and Deliverables

1. Competitive research on ICT markets in Israel, India, Jordan, and Ireland included a review of the following characteristics of these markets:

   - Financial statistics and growth
   - Size
   - Sector breakdown by revenue and cluster activity
   - Industry focus for ICT organizations
   - Impact of education and workforce development initiatives on financial growth
   - Historical patterns and their effect on workforce development
   - Education (to support the industry)
   - Workforce characteristics
   - Size and skills
   - Public institutions
   - Private sector training
   - Entrepreneurial factors' impact on entire industry
   - Availability of finance
   - Demand identification
   - Infrastructure (state of development, technology transfer programs, corporate support)
   - Communications
   - Availability of financial development funds and growth vehicles

- Import and export characteristics
- Domestic demand for ICT sector services
- Skills gap and how it impacts country-level strategy
- Education programs
- National initiatives
- Regional initiatives
- Cluster impact
- Demand generation and sector development patterns
- Comparison of technology skills' gap versus business and supporting skills' gap
- Government support (programs and political initiatives)
- Promotion, marketing, and finance
- Companies and expertise (interviews with four to six firms in country)
- Incubators and private business development

*Deliverable:* Input to the ICT Skills Gap Analysis Report and identification of success factors in other markets. Integration and interpretation of results to be applied to ICT Sector Skills Gap Analysis recommendations.

2. Review of the Egyptian ICT marketplace:

- Collect, review, and access the NWCET skills Standards Classification, and determine the most effective classification system to be used in the project; this also includes collection, review, and assessment of existing ICT skills classification used in research and marketing studies in Egypt, the United States, and other emerging ICT markets (characteristics of these classifications were agreed upon during Phase One of this project)
- Collection of data on existing and emerging organizations in Egypt including, software, telecom, hardware, and related services suppliers
- Financial statistics and growth
- Education (to support the industry)

- Companies and expertise (interviews with 35 to 45 firms in Egypt)
- Estimate of ICT staff by skill category, experience, proficiency level, educational attainment, and professional certification (core competency)

3. Individual organization research:

- Visits to each firm and educational organization based on list agreed upon in Phase One
- Review of business operation and plan
- Review and evaluation of technology or product line, or service offering
- Review of current export plans and strategy
- Discussion of distribution issues for ICT suppliers in the local and international marketplace
- Interviews and analysis based on clusters in segments below:
  - Software companies (6)
  - Hardware companies (2–3)
  - Service providers and consultants to the ICT
  - Telecommunications companies (voice and mobile operators, engineering project implementers) (4)
  - Localization (2)
  - Customer support (call centers) (2)
  - Hardware support (5)
  - Internet service providers (3)
  - Application service providers (3)
  - Customized services (5)
  - Education establishments
  - Public (4)
  - Private (4)
- Capture of Skills Gap Analysis data:
  - By severity of skills gap need
  - Near-term and longer-term needs in the Egyptian ICT sector

- By industry (based on Standard Industry Code classification)
- By skill level and individual skill gap severity

*Deliverable:* Compilation of data to determine current status focusing specifically on how skill gaps are affecting current organizations' effectiveness and their impact on potential future demand or strategy. Include recommendations on technological changes required, necessary changes in skill sets, and modifications needed to improve the quality of product to facilitate and promote exports.

4. ICT Skills Gap Analysis—ICT sector:
   - Report with findings and recommendations including:
     - Skills Gap Analysis in Egyptian ICT Sector
       - By cluster
       - By severity
       - By industry
       - By skill set
       - By certification standards
     - Education and training survey
     - Curriculum that meets ICT sector needs
     - Certification strategies
     - Methods to address skills gaps
     - Curriculum change methods and means
     - Level and types of skills and experience required by the market
     - Ratio to other skill sets to meet ICT sector needs
     - Demand estimate from ICT sector
     - Priority levels for skills and experience
     - Certification requirements
     - Input regarding delivery means acceptable to ICT groups
       - Workshop based

- Experiential (internship, work experience)
- Distance learning

— External country benchmarking and effect on ICT Skills Gap strategy in ICT Sector in Egypt

— Country-specific data and analysis

— Lessons learned

— Strategies that work

— Strategies that did not work

— Recommendations and impact on ICT Egyptian current Skills Gap scenarios

*Deliverable:* Final sector assessment report analyzing the ICT industry strengths, weaknesses, and opportunities. Provide recommendations on future steps with the objective of obtaining a greater share of the international marketplace.

Research instruments with recommendations of how to continue to use existing instruments and measurement spreadsheets for future phases of the project.

5. Trends in regional and international markets: This includes a review of regional and international trends in the relevant market sectors that would have an impact on recommendations from the Skills Gap Analysis data collected in the study. This covered both the telecom and IT segments, which included:

- ICT market size in region (from other studies and sources)
- Growth rates
- Trends that are relevant for future planning in Egyptian ICT sector
- International market-size trends and growth (from other studies)
- Export factors that could impact competitiveness of skills base

## About this Framework

Creating this framework required a variety of project management skills. These skills included research to determine methods and testing, facilitation with the various groups involved in the project, and creation and management of new research teams in Egypt and overseas to capture the relevant research. All of this had to be tightly estimated to ensure that the time lines and data capture were possible. In fact, the testing of the research information instruments ran on several organizations to ensure that the data was obtainable at the appropriate time frame to an acceptable level of quality.

In many complex project plans such as this one, it is not enough to determine deliverables, but in many cases you must also show how each task is going to be handled and clearly illustrate how a goal and an objective are going to be reached. In the business world, there is little of the "trust me" factor when it comes to method, and your customers want to understand how you are going to produce results. For this reason, being able to articulate your project plan in enough detail not only instills confidence, but enables you to gain customers' input to refine the plan.

As all projects at this level are a team sport, there is no other way that ensuring buy-in happens right from the beginning. At the same time, it is important to keep the scope within the borders of what is possible for such projects. The more agendas you have involved in the results, the greater the danger to move off target. What is known as "scope creep" can occur quickly and can render fatal results.

Earlier in the book, we discussed the variable time and how it is used. Scope creep is a time eater and a time waster if you have already agreed on objectives. For example, in the project outlined here, if we started to broaden the questions, the research fields, and the analysis, then we may not have the time to answer the most important questions—the ones that are driving the requirements to reach the goal and objectives. It is easy to get sidetracked and, once there, become derailed.

## Implementation

Once the planning stages were complete and the contract in place, the implementation process began. The plan provided the framework, but there was still other work required to keep the project on schedule. As some research work commenced on the phone, the Web, and through third parties, ensuring that the various phases of the project would come together in the right time required a coordinated effort.

An important factor in making this occur was assuring that the research for the country portion of this project happened while the on-site interviewing occurred in Egypt. This was an important issue for scheduling and allocating appropriate resources.

The on-site project in Egypt required creating a detailed schedule, drafting letters, and executing a large public relations exercise to ensure that the target firms to be interviewed would be willing to take the time and provide the very senior resources that needed to be involved. We were thankful that with some excellent project managers already involved in this sector, setting up the appointments with very busy executives was not as huge a challenge as first seen. However, in the case of this project, it would have been impossible to have organized this from afar without the local connection and network.

Because much of the information that had to be collected was confidential to individual firms, it was important to ensure all data was "blind" as it was compiled and analyzed.

## How It All Worked

The first step in the methodology for this project involved identifying the segments of the ICT sector in which interviews would be conducted with individual companies and industry organizations.

The next critical phase involved developing, reviewing, and agreeing on the methodology and target interviewees to use as the basis for the project. During April 2003, HCG contractors and USAID defined the details of the overall project and approved the methodology and target organizations for interviews.

Next, individual organizations were selected for interviews. The interviews included questions about core capabilities of the firms, export activities, and barriers to success affecting their current performance or plans for export. Also interviewed were industry associations and other bodies that had insight into regulatory issues affecting the ICT sector.

The interviews for the Competitive Analysis program were conducted jointly with another USAID-sponsored project, the *2003 ICT Skills Gap Analysis*. Combining the interviews had the benefit of avoiding many duplicate interviews, making the best use of the participants' valuable time, and saving the project sponsor, USAID, considerable expense for the combined projects.

Data analysis followed completion of the interviews and allowed us to consolidate our findings about the state of the ICT sector in Egypt.

In parallel with the primary research conducted in Egypt, interviews and research were also conducted about the worldwide ICT market and four benchmark countries. After the project team in Cairo selected the four benchmark countries for research, HCG consultants identified potential interview candidates in order to conduct personal interviews with four to six relevant people in each country. We also conducted extensive secondary research on each of the four countries using government, NGO (nongovernmental organizations), and other data sources.

Data from all sources was combined and analyzed to produce the summary findings and analysis on the worldwide ICT market and the benchmark countries.

Finally, combining local and international findings produced recommendations for the Egyptian ICT market, and the first draft of the report was prepared and delivered in August 2003.

## Project Execution

Prior to the start of the project, an initial high-level list of candidate market segments within the Egyptian ICT sector was defined. When the project began, the team refined the list of target segments and identified more specific categories with input from a variety of groups including the contractors and USAID in order to determine the specific focus for the project.

The segments and categories were selected based on the need to sample all areas of the ICT sector. As a result, some segments and categories were included that had only a small number of active organizations, such as call centers and application service providers.

The resulting segment and category list is shown below. Numbers in parentheses represent the number of organizations that needed to be interviewed to create an accurate and useful consensus for the Competitive Analysis.

- Software companies (11)

- Hardware companies (3)

- Service providers and consultants to the ICT
    - Arabization and culturization (3)
    - Customer support (call centers) (3)
    - Hardware support (6)
    - Internet service providers (3)
    - Application service providers (3)
    - Customized services (12)

- Telecommunications companies (voice operators, mobile operators, and engineering project implementers) (5)

- Governmental regulatory advisors and industry associations (5)

- Education and training establishments
    - Public (4)
    - Private (4)

Phase Two of the process consisted of selecting and ensuring an appropriate sample set of firms to create a good cross section of the ICT sector. Fifty-seven organizations were selected to meet the requirements of the Competitive Analysis Project.

## Setting Up the Interview Questions and Data Capture

Once the industry segmentation and categorizations were complete and interview candidates selected, interview questions and data capture tools for the study were developed. As each interview needed to provide insight into the company's operations, markets, revenue performance, and growth factors, it was critically important that the right staff members were present and interview requirements understood in advance.

As the data capture for this project was run in parallel with the Skills Gap Analysis, the interviews were typically broken into two segments, a business segment discussing the overall characteristics of the operation followed by the Skills Gap Analysis segment.

Attendees in each of these meetings included the CEO and/or managing director, marketing and sales management, technical management (development and support), and HR managers where appropriate. In some cases the size of the organization (e.g., Telecom Egypt) warranted multiple meetings to capture relevant data.

During each meeting we reviewed the goals for the studies and assured all participants that they would gain the aggregate information from the two studies being conducted as a result of the data collection. We also indicated that the Egyptian Ministry for Communications and Information Technology supported the program and USAID sponsored it, and that any information collected at an individual firm level would not be shared outside of the interview and data collection process. Only aggregated data would be compiled and included in the finished report(s).

At the beginning of each interview, we outlined the skills and roles categorization that we were using and indicated that it was based on industry standards with extensions in the skills identification section. We also outlined the segments and categories that we were measuring for the ICT sector.

The introductory segment typically took 15 to 20 minutes before any data collection could start. Data collection consisted of capturing information from predefined questions that included the following topics:

- Total revenue for 2002
- Revenue generated from direct sales
- Revenue generated from distribution partnerships or other channels
- Revenue from the domestic market
- Revenue from the regional market—the Middle East and North Africa (MENA)
- Revenue from the rest of the world (primarily the United States and Europe)

Follow-up questions then included their perception of what differentiates them in their target markets, including

- their unique selling proposition(s) (USP), and
- their competitive positioning in target markets.

We then moved to questions regarding factors related to economic conditions, export barriers, local market supporting services, and educational issues in order to identify challenges their organizations face in the domestic and export marketplaces.

Final questions captured any other issues or recommendations that the company might have had that would improve the competitiveness of their operations.

In the majority of cases, firms provided adequate information; however, a few firms were reluctant to provide revenue or detailed numbers.

The interview process for all organizations was conducted from April 2003 through July 2003. After data capture in Egypt was completed, the analysis process began.

## Data Analysis from the Interview Process

Once the interviews were complete, data about each firm's core technical, marketing, sales, revenue, and staffing levels was compiled into the relevant industry segments and categories. Maps illustrating core competencies and the maturity of the domestic and export markets for each segment were prepared using the consolidated data.

Revenue and employment data from each segment were compiled and analyzed to determine segment size and productivity. Selected data was interpolated to ensure that revenue streams would not inflate or distort results from the study. For example, many of the customized application providers sell hardware as a part of their solutions, so an estimated percentage of the hardware component was subtracted from that overall revenue estimate.

We believe that the bottom-up approach used in this study represented the most detailed revenue analysis of the ICT sector ever conducted in Egypt. Further, because this study is based on direct interviews and scrutiny of business operations data from dozens of firms, we believe the results are more accurate than estimates made with a top-down approach.

## Research on the ICT Markets and Country-Level Benchmarking

For the country benchmark research, USAID selected four countries that have been successful in exporting ICT services or that are actively developing an export industry. Table 7.2 summarizes the reasons India, Israel, Jordan, and the Philippines were selected.

TABLE 7.2 *Selected Benchmark Countries*

| COUNTRY | REASON FOR INCLUSION |
|---|---|
| India | • Has become an ICT-outsourcing powerhouse<br>• Is the reference point for many maturing countries wishing to develop an export industry but starting with limited infrastructure |
| Israel | • Has developed and distributed high-quality products and intellectual property<br>• Has a relatively small ICT workforce but generates extremely high revenue per employee<br>• Provides location similar to Egypt's, though many other characteristics are substantially different |
| Jordan | • Small country with small ICT workforce but is currently developing its ICT sector<br>• Moving quickly so may be useful to learn from its recent actions<br>• Has similar geographic and cultural characteristics, focused on high-value export activities |
| Philippines | • Very large population, though vastly smaller than India<br>• Extremely literate population with excellent English language skills<br>• Not a powerhouse in ICT export, though government has placed significant emphasis on building a call-center industry in recent years |

Once the four countries had been identified, the statement of work for this project outlined the specific categories for which data was needed. Research on the ICT markets and country-level benchmarking was completed by using sources such as *The Global Information Technology Report* and *Digital Planet 2002*, as well as other reports, white papers, and publications. For the country-level benchmarking, data from the World Bank, the Asian Development Bank, the United Nations, the International Telecommunications Union, and other international organizations augmented economic statistics and development plans published by the countries themselves.

TABLE 7.3 *Analysis Criteria for ICT Market Segments*

| SEGMENT | IN-COUNTRY SKILLS | EXPORT POTENTIAL | MARKET SUCCESS | RANKING |
|---|---|---|---|---|
| | Technical skills | Knowledge of market(s) | Demonstrated success domestically | |
| | Management skills | Cultural compatibility | Demonstrated success with multinationals active in target market(s) | The analysis and rankings for each segment was based on the compilation of these factors. |
| | Marketing skills | Knowledge of segment(s) | Demonstrated success in target export market(s) | Given that in-country skills in most categories would be a requirement for success, there would still need to be a high score for export potential and market success in order to score high overall. |
| (Segment names here) | Industry-specific skills | Financial wherewithal | Presence in target market for more than 24 months | |
| | | Partners | | |
| | | Competitiveness of offerings | | |

Supporting these official sources, a collection of news articles, press releases, and other reports validated and substantiated the data. Finally, personal interviews with technology company executives, government officials, researchers, and advisors in the benchmarking countries filled knowledge gaps, pointed to new data sources, and validated information and assumptions.

## Analyzing Local and International Findings and Developing the Recommendations

Once the local and international analyses were complete, the next step was to analyze the impact of both sets of findings together and determine the recommendations for next steps for the ICT sector.

The first stage of this process used the core competency and market maturity maps to estimate the Egyptian ICT sector's potential success (or failure) based on current and future market conditions.

The analysis also included a ranking by segment of in-country skills, export potential, and market success in either domestic or export markets. By way of example, the table below illustrates the different consideration factors determining the overall ranking for each segment.

## Project Management

Even though this very complex project needed to be managed carefully, it is also obvious that the principles outlined in our earlier chapters helped us gain an excellent outcome. In this particular project, the outcome shows a direct relationship between the quality of the information and the voluntary participation of larger numbers of senior executives. Fortunately, in this case I had some earlier experience with some of the participants, but others were new.

Fraught with risk, this project was successful only because of a very tight definition of the goals and objectives, and agreement of the methodology used to reach conclusions. Rather like an engineering design project, providing transparency to the manufacturing or creative process was very important to getting others to buy in.

Figure 7.3 illustrates how flowcharts and visual aids can again help in that process. In the case of this particular project, showing the application of the project research in the decision-making process required using this diagram time and time again. Showing this *methodology* was imperative to

FIGURE 7.3 *Project Methodology*

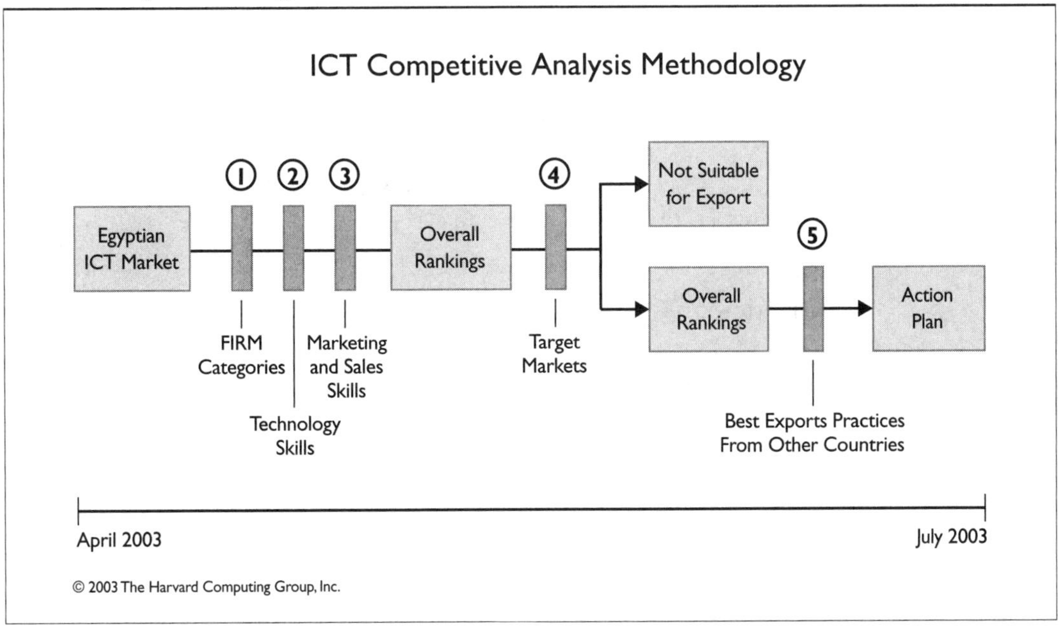

gaining confidence in the project process and demonstrating that the result would be a successful analysis and interpretation of the information.

Once recommendations for geographic market penetration and individual target markets were identified, the best practices resulting from the analysis of the country-level research were used to prepare recommendations for actionable items to improve Egyptian ICT Exports.

## Best Practices

This project illustrates the need for many of the tools and techniques outlined in earlier chapters. Communication with team members, facilitation, workshops, meeting management, and analysis skills all came together to produce a good result.

The project met the on-time and on-budget requirements of the owners, despite the challenges laid out at the outset. Projects with time-sensitive outcomes need continual management and attention. If the time frames start to move, then the relevancy of project decisions and assumptions can also change. This is particularly true of technology-oriented projects where market conditions, costs, and availability of participants continually change.

# PROJECT THREE—SETTING UP A TRADE SHOW

## The Plan

Our third and final sample project is planning and setting up a trade show. Setting up and running a trade show event or booth is a frequent requirement for many first-time project managers. This might be a small event at a local hotel or something more challenging, depending on your job roles. Before making the decision of which event to attend, some research is required, namely setting the goals and objectives for your organization's attendance at the event.

The goals and objectives may be a specific number of inquiries of individuals at a certain level, so an initial review of the various events helps determine your selection. In addition, the budget factors play heavily into this decision process.

However, before you reach this point, review the trade show demographics to determine whether they meet your target audience criteria. These may include

- who attends the trade show;
- how many people attend and who they are—business managers, purchasers, IT technicians, project managers, retailers, or wholesalers;
- who else has a booth at this trade show—your competition; and
- what the visibility of the booth is.

## The Budget

Because budgeting for trade shows is usually not a one-time event but rather part of a systematic sales and marketing plan, review each show in context for its contribution to the overall budget. Questions that help you come to the right conclusions in this area include the following:

- How many trade shows do you plan on attending in one year?
- What percentage of your overall marketing dollars are you prepared to allocate to trade shows?
- What is the estimated return on the investment?

In some cases a trade show event may run in connection with other events, such as conferences and educational programs for the target audiences. Sometimes an opportunity to present at one of these events bolsters the overall benefits of the event, as you gain the ability to create both leads and industry image advertising. In the other forums, there may be opportunities for sponsorship, further increasing visibility.

Assuming that the event has the potential to generate the type and quality of leads you are pursuing, the next stage is calculating the budget.

**Calculating the Budget Line Items.** Calculate the budget using estimated cost requirements from the show organization and supporting marketing and sales expenses:

1. Booth cost—Includes the actual cost of the booth and all sundry expenses such as electricity, booth displays, rental costs, union fees for staff at the conference, carpeting, and so on
2. Literature costs—Brochures, signage
3. Travel and entertainment expenses—Airfare and hotel for the number of attendees from your company
4. Equipment and product shipping expenses
5. Cost of entertaining and dining customers and prospects

Once the estimate has been made and the anticipated return on investment meets the required criteria, the next stage occurs: planning the event.

## Planning Ahead

Most trade shows have registration open at least six months in advance, sometimes even earlier. This is important as the best booths are reserved immediately and care needs to be taken to ensure you are in the most appropriate traffic patterns for your products or service. Timing is important, for late sign-ups often forfeit inclusion in show directories and the like, further reducing your visibility to attendees using these documents to plan their time at the show.

As many of the leading shows do sell out—sometimes for years in advance—don't let a waiting list put you off. Stay in contact with the show representatives; it is not unknown for booths to become available at the last moment.

The example illustrated here shows a firm that was initially told it would take approximately seven years on the waiting list to gain a booth at the New York Gift Show, a major retailing show. By keeping in contact with the show representative and emphasizing awareness that the firm would be the show catalog, the firm was still willing to attend and could at a day's notice. This last-minute technique worked, and the firm had a very productive show and priority on entry to the show the following year.

Booth placement is important. Review with trade show management the layout of the show and the traffic patterns. Inquire who is located in booths on either side of yours. (There's no need to have the competition breathing down your neck.) Best locations are often near the entrances, a corner booth, or just near the lunch/snack locations where attendees congregate in numbers.

FIGURE 7.4 *Setting Up and Managing a Trade Show*

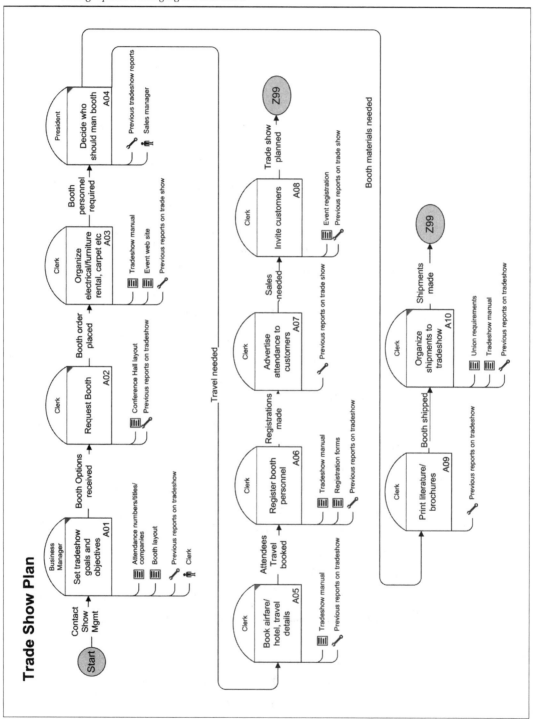

## More Planning and Checklists Guidelines

Once you have purchased your booth at the trade show, the work begins.

1. Advertise—Notify all your customers of your location and make your company visible. Not only will this help if they plan on attending, but if they are not attending, it still gives good touch points with the client/customer.

2. Preplan—Be aware that all trade shows have deadlines for electrical and furniture rentals, and after the deadlines the prices become exorbitant. For the electrical planning keep in mind that you will need lighting and the more the better. If you have computers, you will require access to electrical power, particularly if you have a demonstration workstation.

3. Shipping—Many shows are union run; shipping has to be arranged with approved shippers.

4. You will need to review the trade show handbook to ensure that you have covered the setup and dismantling of the booth. Many shows require booth authorization. Sometimes you can ship UPS, DHL, FedEx, or one of these similar services directly to the show. There could be a charge for the box delivery to the booth. Remember to always mark all shipments with the booth number.

5. Booth décor—How large is the booth? How high are the back and sides? What color is the drape? When considering decorating, light and bright should be high in your thinking.

6. Review the items included with the booth—do not assume that carpet, tables, chairs, or even a trash can is included. Remember that it is highly likely that not only will you have to preorder carpet and booth furniture but will also have to pay for daily vacuuming and trash collection. If the booth is not too large, it may be a good idea to include a small tablecloth cleaner in your booth supplies so that you can avoid the vacuuming charges. A small, prepackaged, fold-up wastebasket can save money.

7. Review setup and plan accordingly—Remember that if you require only a few hours to set up, then there is no need to send employees out to the show for the entire setup time allocated, as the company may incur unnecessary additional hotel expenses.

8. Product displays—Check with the show's management to find the display area for products, another marketing tool for the company. Large gift shows invariably have an area allocated to new products, and you can request to have products displayed there.

9. Literature—Always bring at least one original of any piece of literature. In the event that you run out of brochures, then at least you can have them copied.

10. Giveaways—Some trade shows have giveaways; register in advance for these. Normally for the show attendees to be in the drawing for these, they have to sign up at your booth. This can be another incentive or draw for obtaining more visibility. Ideas for the giveaway could be a product or service from your company.

11. Speaking slots—Arrange these in advance. This is another key way of attracting customers and introducing them to your product. Many trade shows will not only

have major speakers but will also have smaller areas allocated for demonstrations.

12. Personnel—Ensure show management has the form showing employees who will be on the booth and who is the contact person in attendance at the show.

13. Travel arrangements—If you are a smaller company still trying to save money on travel, try:

— *www.priceline.com*
— *www.hotels.com*
— *www.hotwire.com*
— *www.orbitz.com*
— *www.travelocity.com*
— *www.site59.com*
— *www.itasoftware.com*

Sites like these can save you expenses on both airfares and hotels. The show manual normally will have approved hotels with discounted rooms available to show attendees. These need to be prebooked to obtain the better rates.

14. Shuttle service—Many of the approved hotels accommodate the free shuttle that many of the larger conventions provide to and from the convention center. This can be another great savings idea.

## Implement—Booth Design and Setup

If your company has a technology focus and the trade show is dependent on many demonstrations, make sure that the lighting is effective. At a minimum, spend on a decent sign—something that will let everyone know exactly what your product does for them and reinforces your brand and message. This draws the future customer in. Be sure demonstration tables are in the front of the booth. Have some eye-catching information displayed on the computer monitors explaining your product's functionality and benefits. Include references from existing customers if possible. Have plenty of literature available and evaluation materials relevant to your business.

In the wholesale/distribution business again, lighting is very important. If possible, utilize your product as a display vehicle. Be sure that your literature amply describes your product, has stunning pictures and pricing information, and, if possible, an example of uses for the product. Know that event attendees leave each convention with so much literature that very often yours can get lost in the shuffle.

A good-looking booth does not necessarily cost a fortune. Many booths are extremely costly and created so that they can fit only one booth design. If you purchase a booth, check to see if it can be changed or expanded as the company grows.

## Managing the Show

Once at the show, take the following steps to keep the management of the booth on track:

1. Register with the show staff and obtain any relevant new information that the staff might have. Make sure all the necessary employees are on the registration list.

2. Visit the booth and ascertain whether you have everything that you have ordered. Each show has an area where you can obtain electrical hookups or additional booth furniture and so on. For instance, gift shows always have hooks from which to hang signs, and these are usually free.

3. Check that all your shipments have arrived. Normally, all packages are delivered directly to the booth for setup. Now is the time to check for any missing items. Items sometimes are delivered to the wrong booth.

4. Set up the booth. Make sure the electrical layout is sufficient for demonstration tables and so on. Never leave any computer equipment out at a show—theft is a major problem, even with security present during the nonexhibit hours.

5. Place some cloth to cover the stand, products, and tables when you leave the show in the evening. Pack away and conceal all monitors and so on.

6. Plan to bring all laptops back to the hotel each evening.

## Important Employee Information and Briefing Sessions

Set up a briefing meeting and review each day to ensure that you get the best from the event. The list of tasks includes these:

1. Plan a meeting designating who is responsible for setup.

2. Meet prior to the trade show opening to reinforce the objectives and goals for the show.

3. Agree on how you are going to work together. If the booth is small, it is even more important to know who is going to do what, when you should take breaks, and how many staff members should be on the stand at any one point. How important is it to mingle and visit the other booths? Is it important to do some target marketing at the show? Are there other companies whom you should

be considering as partners and how much importance do you want to place on that at this show? Should anybody be attending any of the sessions that often are going on during exhibit hours, and, if so, what is the expectation from these sessions? Clarify all these points so that staff clearly understands what their roles are and how they should be executed for the duration of the event.

4. At the end of each day, summarize the achievements and list the objectives for the following day based on the results of the day and staff input.

5. If necessary, lay out times that are convenient for scheduling personalized appointments for customers with the technical staff, sales, or other management from the company.

6. Review any issues that have occurred and also make sure that there is still plenty of literature available. There is almost always a local fast copy shop near the convention area or hotel. The show staff will have that information.

## After the Show

Many firms do not do a great job of following up after events, which is a real shame. In many cases there are weeks of preparation for events, expenses, and a huge investment in time. This effort has to be leveraged, and one way of doing this is ensuring that a follow-up plan is in place for leads generated as a result of the event. Rarely do we have the opportunity to present products to such a wide range of individuals as at a trade show, so take their input, both positive and negative. This will help you for your next event, changes to the product line, and competitive information in your chosen sector.

## SUMMARY

It is worth noting that although these three projects were of a very different order of magnitude, the steps for each were the same. Terminology about the project and project status are identical; only the sophistication and application of the three-step process differed. The same can be said of all projects despite their size and complexity.

It is noticeable that the more complex a project, the more important it is to ensure that participants and project owners have a good visual clue as to what is happening. Making an investment to make certain that these diagrams and documents are prepared and distributed will pay big dividends.

Even more important, as things change, you must keep your project team up-to-date. Remember, things can be changed if you communicate. Things won't change if you don't tell your team.

# 8

# WHEN THINGS GO WRONG— TROUBLESHOOTING

*"The happy and efficient people in this world are those who accept trouble as a normal detail of human life and resolve to capitalize on it when it comes along."*

**H. Bertram Lewis**

Sooner or later some aspect of a project starts to come undone. Deadlines advancing too quickly, budgets getting out of control, team members concerned about quality: all factors that need attention.

Even as a new project manager, the first reaction to trouble should not be blind panic. Every project will have stages when things are likely to go wrong, even if it is just the weather not cooperating with a building project. Getting used to this is one of the first steps toward effective project management.

## WHAT CAN GO WRONG

There are usually four categories of things that go wrong with a project: budget problems, quality, missed deadlines, and market conditions making your project unnecessary or no longer compelling.

FIGURE 8.1 *Project Troublemaking Items and Their Relationship to the Project Cycle*

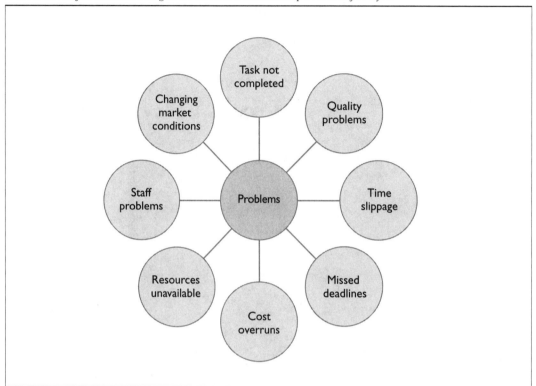

*Expect some level of difficulty*
*with almost every project.*

Don't be surprised if you encounter some of these problems in the course of your project. Expect some level of difficulty with almost every project. The exceptions of course are when projects have an unlimited budget, very flexible time lines, or a very drawn-out schedule.

The more aggressive projects are usually the ones that have the best managers working with them.

## Looking Out for Trouble

Staying on top of the project schedule and status is obviously one way of ensuring that problems come to light as early as possible. If they're noticed as they emerge, it is always easier to deal with difficulties and developing problems. The best project managers *look* for trouble before it starts—rather like a doctor prescribing preventive advice before something more serious kicks in.

# DEALING WITH TROUBLE

The first step when trouble comes knocking is to take five. Listen to what the problem is . . . Then, long before reacting, take some time to determine the severity. Examine the problem; determine its impact on the project; and then start to develop an action plan. Do not panic. Don't overreact and, above all, don't overreact in front of the project team or the individual who may have brought this bad news to your attention. On that point, do not "shoot the messenger" either, as he or she may never bring bad news to your attention again.

Sometimes problems arise because some members of the project team do not see all of the activities or the progress being made. Lack of communication with the team is often the cause and, as discussed in earlier chapters, is completely avoidable. If this is the problem, then you, as project manager, are the problem. Fortunately this is a relatively easy one to fix.

## Listen and Assess

Listening is defined as "hearing with attention." I like that definition because some project managers hear but don't listen to what is being communicated. In some cases the individual may also be nervous about bringing this news to you and therefore may emphasize certain parts of the problem and not others. This is one reason why an initial reaction to the issue should be avoided if possible.

> *Listening is defined as "hearing with attention."*

For example, a team member may let you know that a deadline is going to be missed and that the primary cause of this is another person or vendor not delivering what the person or vendor needs. After you listen to the issue and examine all factors, you may find that the problem is more likely half the vendor's problem and half the other team member's problem. If you immediately react to the message that the vendor is late, the fact that your team member did not provide the vendor with an earlier deliverable may have caused the problem in the first place.

> *"Nature has given us two ears but only one mouth."*
> Benjamin Disraeli

This is an important point in project management; if your team members know that you react badly to bad news, they will try to avoid *delivering* it to you. My earlier point of shooting the messenger applies here. As a project manager, you want all the news about the project, both good and bad. This is needed to take the necessary action when issues arise.

Once the problem is known, then take the necessary time to assess its impact on the project. By determining the severity of the issue, the action plan that results may differ considerably.

## Determine an Action Plan

Once the severity of the problem has been determined, you need to build an action plan to solve the issue. Your action plan's contents will vary depending on the significance of the change. For minor changes, increased resources, staff, or some parallel process activities might provide the results. More significant changes require taking more drastic actions. Typical plans could include

- minor course correction within scope of existing plan;

- significant impact on current budget or deadlines—build document change and agree on revised project plan with changes factored in; or

- huge impact on plan—rebudgeting or assessing the viability of the current project may be in order.

Once this assessment is made, prepare for action whatever the level of change involved.

FIGURE 8.2 *Action Plan Process Options*

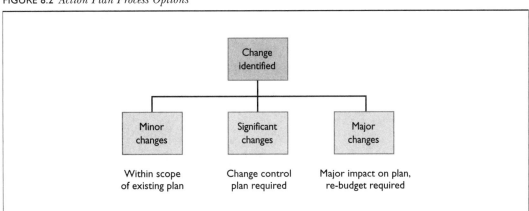

## Take Action

Some project managers are good at listening and even planning but seem reluctant to take action. Like jumping off the diving board or going down a ski slope for the first time, or taking on any first-time challenge—you must take action.

*"In the arena of human life*
*the honors and rewards fall to those*
*who show their good qualities in action."*

Aristotle

No amount of research or planning takes the place of someone's doing something. If the investment has already been made to resolve the problem, then just do it. Ensure that the action plan includes communication with all team members, not just those impacted by the changes. At times of trouble, overcommunication can help motivate the team to take on the new challenges and give new life to the project. Action steps should include the following:

- Communicate the plan to get the project back on track
- Determine specific actions for individuals or groups
- Ensure all members understand the impact on the current plan and schedule
- Slow down or stop activities that may be affected

*No amount of research or planning*
*takes the place of someone's*
*doing something.*

# STAYING IN CONTROL—CHANGE CONTROL

One way to avoid disruptive change in a project is to embrace it. Embrace it? Yes. When schedules are changing as a result of project scope adjustments or other resources or factors outside your purview, manage the issue. Controlling change is one of the most important aspects of any project, and using a strategy and means keeps trouble at bay.

## Changing Requirements and Needs

Have you ever been running something where the requirements seem to constantly keep changing? This can be particularly frustrating when this happens once a project is under way. Sometimes the requirements change after a project starts because of poor planning. It could be that issue research lacked detail, project tasks and processes now differ considerably from the project plan, or the client is changing his or her goals and objectives.

Whatever the reason for these changes, it is essential as project manager that you bring order to the chaos. From the initial planning and acceptance stage of a project, it is very important that the project owner or sponsor be willing to accept that changes in scope be subject to a change control process from the beginning.

The change control process may need to be fairly sophisticated where many changes need to be managed during the life of a project. As an example, developing a software product has many differing stages and always has some form of change control involved during its development cycle. These may be as a result of user feedback during testing of the product, interface changes, functional differences, or integration with other systems not initially considered.

For all of these reasons, it is imperative the *change control* process be agreed on from the start. That way all involved in the project know what is likely to happen when something needs to be changed.

## When Something Has to Change

> *"There is always a way to do things better. Find it."*
> Thomas Edison

Candidates for the change control process start by identifying what needs to be changed. Depending on the severity of the change and its impact on the project, there can be different actions. For example, if someone were out of work for a single day because of illness, and it has no material impact on the project, it would be noted but no action would be taken.

Conversely, a software development project where a critical function is required for the project's success could be grounds for a change control process to begin.

The following are issues that could cause a change control process to kick in:

- Unbudgeted increases in resources or staff
- Changes in time frames or deadlines
- New or significantly changed functionality
- Unforeseen market condition changes

Each of these points alone would be enough to initiate a change control process. If there is a combination of them, it might mean a major review of the project. Some organizations will even have a series of guidelines to determine what sets up a change control process: a certain level of increases in costs; time frames moved more than a week; a new competitor in the market. Whatever the applicable trigger, agreement should be in advance of the project start. Once a candidate for change has been noted, then raise the flag with your project owner or sponsor.

## Managing Changes in the Project

Once the change or trouble has been identified, a strict and agreed-upon process needs to start immediately. Imagine how many projects are started—the project owner signs the contract, and the project manager begins work. Everyone assumes that all is going to go perfectly through the process, the project owner or his or her sponsor never changing his or her mind or project needs and the project manager never changing anything or missing any deadlines.

It's the stuff that dreams are made of but unfortunately not how it typically happens. What is amazing is the number of project managers who enter a project and never discuss how they are going to deal with changes. This very obvious and big *mistake* is one made not just by novice project managers but by experienced managers as well. Trust me and all will be well. It is truly amazing how many times this mistake is made.

Once the decision to start a change control process is made, the following three actions should take place:

1. Draft a change control document outlining

   a. what changes are going to occur;

   b. impact on budget, time frames, and deadlines; and

   c. time frame for the change review.

2. Agree on a change control process to include

   a. how and when the change control document will be reviewed;

   b. negotiation procedures; and

   c. the change control process.

3. Start the change control process.

As Figure 8.3 illustrates, the change management process determines exactly how changes will be accepted and integrated into the existing project plan. This single technique provides both the project owner and the project management team a means to deal with change in the project successfully. Without this mechanism in the program, it would be impossible to deal with changes, which in turn leads to disputes and more.

## Modifying the Plan

The result of these changes is the modification of the plan as well as its implementation and management. Each of these changes and their potential impact on the project should be documented and integrated as soon as practical.

Depending on the amount of change, deadlines and the impact on the project time lines may require modification. Keeping a project on schedule is important, but if the current plan is not going to create a successful result for the client,

FIGURE 8.3 *Change Management Process*

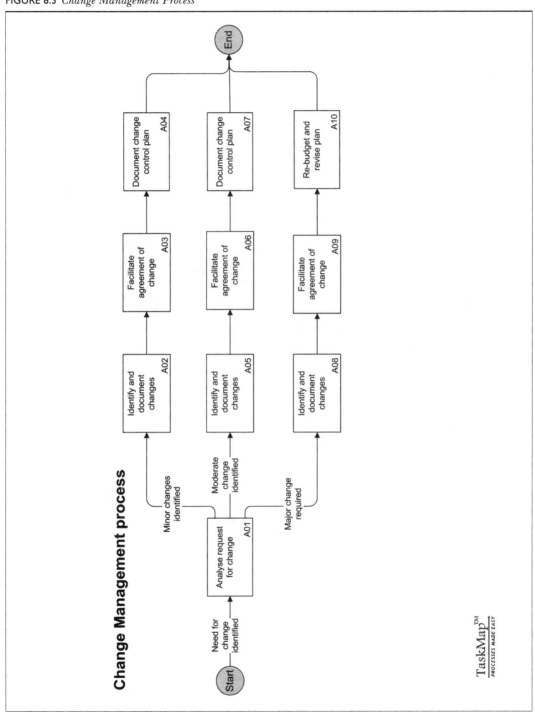

then changing it to meet revised needs is better than delivering an undesirable result on schedule.

Changes to the plan should reflect not just a change itself but also its impact on other affected deadlines or dependencies.

# REBUDGETING

In the most severe of changes to the project, there may be the need to rebudget all or part of the project. If the scope or the time lines of a project change significantly, it may make sense to provide a revised budget for the entire program.

When doing so, note the impact on current resources, staff levels, and the contracts that are already in place with the current vendors on the project. Use a checklist such as the one below to avoid missing important points.

- Scope of changes documented in change control plan
- Impact on current resource estimates
- Cost changes for staff allocation
- Timing impact on delivery, payments, and penalties
- Review of current contracts and their schedules
- Effect on quality standards set for the project

Reviewing a checklist such as this assists in making sure that nothing is missed in the rebudgeting process. This varies according to the approval characteristics of the current project.

For example, if the current project permits an up to 10 percent increase in cost without rebudgeting, there may be no need to go through the approval process, although it is still critical to note and circulate the cost changes to the project owners.

## DON'T TAKE IT PERSONALLY

As difficulties arise with projects, it is often hard not to take them personally. After all, the buck has to stop somewhere, and the project manager is a logical place. Rather than taking it personally, make the project and getting it back on track the most important issues.

> *"To wear your heart on your sleeve*
> *isn't a very good plan; you should wear it inside,*
> *where it functions best."*
>
> Margaret Thatcher

Separating the personal from the project also helps to deal with other team members. Rather than admonishing them for the problem, work with them to resolve it and get it back on track. Most individuals have a pretty good idea when they have made a mess of something anyway. Work done badly is hard to hide and defending its quality even more difficult. So move on, and help the team get to the next step—bringing the project back in line.

# 9

# TEN SUREFIRE WAYS
# TO GET YOUR PROJECT DONE
# ON TIME AND ON BUDGET

These ten shortcuts will help you en-sure that *every* project is an on-time and on-budget event. Each of the *surefire ways* will help you see if your current project is under control and assist you in ways to regain control if it's not. I explain why each way should be important to your project and provide best practices for you to take action im-mediately. Use this short checklist to better manage even ex-isting projects today.

## I. SET ACHIEVABLE GOALS AND OBJECTIVES

*"A dream is just a dream.*
*A goal is a dream with a plan and a deadline."*

Harvey Mackay

FIGURE 9.1 *Surefire Rule #1: Set Achievable Goals and Objectives*

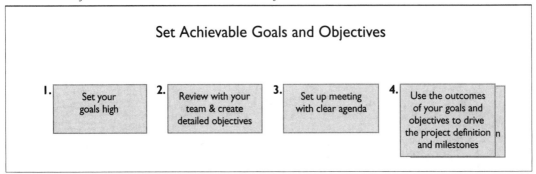

There is no way that any project will have the expected outcome unless agreeing to and setting goals and objectives. Sure, there will always be the accidental discovery or success, such as Post-it® notes or penicillin, but if you want to ensure success, then set goals and objectives.

## Why

Imagine a project that does not have well-defined goals and objectives. Does one come to mind? We have all been a part of such endeavors; sometimes they come out with moderate results, but more often than not they produce what was defined—a variable and flexible set of outcomes and surefire way to reduce your success.

Individuals often shy away from this first step because it also means potential conflict, facilitation, negotiation, compromise, research, among many other things. However, avoiding the issue entirely or making up your own goals and objectives without the participation of others involved surely affects the potential for results.

## Surefire Practice

1. *Set your high-level goals.* First of all, create a short list of items that represent your high-level goals. These might be to increase sales, increase margins, or improve sales productivity.

2. *Review with the team and create detailed objectives.* Review these with the members of the team who would likely be able to effect these goals or, at the very least, be responsible for delivering the improved results. For example, set up a brainstorming meeting with an agenda to review ideas to increase sales productivity or margins. Invite those who can help.

3. Set an agenda for the meeting that includes the following:

   a. Meeting purpose and expected outcomes

   b. Overview and attendees' roles

   c. High-level goal-setting sessions

   d. Objectives to support those goals

   e. Prioritization of identified goals and objectives

   f. Summary and next steps

4. Use the outcomes of your goals and objectives to drive the project definition and milestones.

# 2. LOOK OUT FOR TROUBLE—EMPLOY PROACTIVE MANAGEMENT

Assumption is known as the mother of all foul-ups and nowhere is that more true than in managing a project. Proactive management of any project will save your project time and time again.

> *"The secret of getting ahead is getting started.*
> *The secret of getting started is breaking your*
> *complex overwhelming tasks into small manageable*
> *tasks, and then starting on the first one."*
>
> Mark Twain

## Why

Whatever the reason, taking your eye off the ball during a project always causes problems. The amount of malfeasance only varies according to how much negligence has occurred.

FIGURE 9.2 *Surefire Rule #2: Look Out for Trouble–Employ Proactive Management*

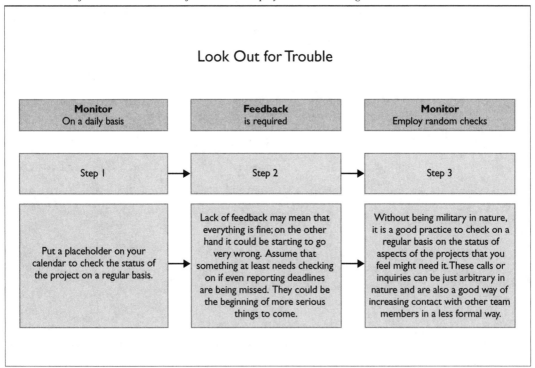

## Surefire Practice

1. *Monitor what is happening every day.* Put a placeholder on your calendar to check the status of the project on a regular basis.

2. *If project members are not providing feedback, do not assume that nothing is wrong.* Lack of feedback may mean that everything is fine; on the other hand it could be starting to go badly wrong. Assume that something at least needs checking on if even reporting deadlines are missed. It could be the beginning of more sinister things to come.

3. *Employ a policy of random checks.* Without being military in nature, it is a good practice to check, on a regular basis, the status of aspects of the project that you feel might need it. These calls or inquiries can be just arbitrary and are a good way of increasing contact with other team members less formally.

# 3. MAKE A PLAN AND THEN FOLLOW THROUGH

*"We succeed only as we identify in life,*
*or in war, or in anything else,*
*a single overriding objective, and make all other*
*considerations bend to that one objective."*

Dwight D. Eisenhower

Sometimes the simplest things are the ones we miss, and when we look at some of the problems that arise during a complex project, it is easy to waver from the initial plan and framework in place.

FIGURE 9.3 *Surefire Rule #3: Make a Plan and Then Follow Through*

- *Build the plan and then follow it*
  - Stick to it
  - Implement quickly
- *Once the plan is in place, implement it around those rules*
  - Don't change the rules unless you have to
  - Try and avoid getting derailed
- *Manage as if your career depended on it*
  - In most cases it just might
  - Stay focused

## Why

The project management framework in this book is deliberately simple. If you want to keep your project on track, then simply refer to it. Whatever state or stage your project is in, there is no doubt it is at one of these three steps. Others involved in your project will also not have *any* difficulty understanding where they fit into the picture.

## Surefire Practice

1. *Build the plan and then follow it.* Sounds obvious, but if you start with a plan but then don't follow it, what was the point? Otherwise, why did you go to all the trouble of estimating, gaining agreement, setting schedules, budgeting, and gaining approval only to deviate? Implement the

plan as quickly as is possible after approval, unless of course the project owner or sponsor has gotten cold feet or wants to change the scope.

2. *Once the plan is in place, implement it around those rules.* Implementing the plan should use all of the start-up project skills and materials discussed in Chapter 4. The second step is often the hardest, particularly when it is your first time managing a big program.

3. *Manage as if your career depended on it.* Treating even the smaller projects energetically and with enthusiasm gets you noticed. Often doing those projects well leads to increases in responsibility and greater challenges in the future. Build on those steps.

# 4. WATCH THE CLOCK

*"Do not delay;*
*Do not delay;*
*the golden moments fly!"*

Henry Wadsworth Longfellow

"Time keeps on ticking, ticking, ticking . . . right into the *future,*" sang Steve Miller. Never were truer words spoken about life and project management. That clock just keeps on running and it's your job to make sure it does not run out of sand before you finish the project.

FIGURE 9.4 *Surefire Rule #4: Watch the Clock*

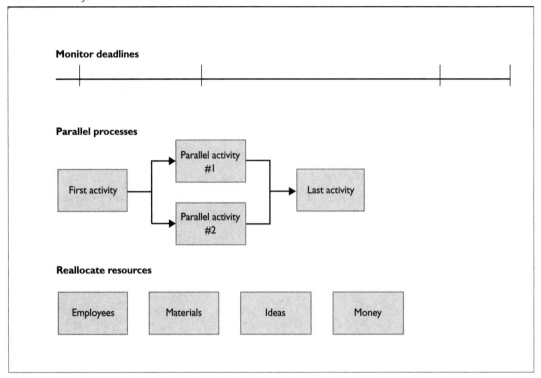

## Why

Time management is one of the simple rules for project management. Someone wants and expects the job done in a certain time frame. Once late, you have missed the mark. Time is one variable that isn't going to change unless your project scope or deadlines are moved with full knowledge and permission. For most, being late is what it is—late. No amount of excuses or reasons can alter the fact. Once the project is late, it's late, and it just becomes a matter of how late. No prizes are awarded for giving that news to your project sponsor or owner.

## Surefire Practice

1. *Worry about and manage your deadlines.* It is not enough to just manage your deadlines; good project managers worry about missing them. Project management, just as any other set of skills, is enhanced when we take the performance of these duties personally. Individuals who don't worry about being on time for meetings or making arrangements and continually changing them make poor project managers. This is not because they could not change their behavior, but because they don't worry enough about the impact of their untimely results.

2. *Parallel activities.* Once time starts to become a problem in the project, immediately consider actions to change the course so that deadlines or budgets are not affected adversely. One excellent method to deal with this is to start activities on a parallel track. This can help to accelerate other parts of the project to make up for the time lags that have already occurred.

3. *Move resources.* Another means to deal with time and deadline problems is to move resources and staff from one part of the project to another. In the most severe of cases this might mean increasing budgets or altering the scope of goals or objectives. Depending on the value of time to this project these still might be worth considering.

# 5. WATCH THE BUDGET

Watched pots may never boil, but unwatched budgets do. Keeping a keen eye on your budget saves you surprises throughout any successful project.

FIGURE 9.5 *Surefire Rule #5: Watch the Budget*

---

**Budget-Related Issues**

- Keep budget information transparent
- Monitor cost controls
- Don't trade off quality for time

---

## Why

Once costs are out of control, it becomes more and more difficult to deliver outcomes from the project with any success factor. Proactive monitoring of costs and time frames associated with the budget always produces big dividends, even though this often is an area that many of us don't like visiting.

## Surefire Practice

1. *Keep the budget information transparent to those who need it.* Make sure that the budget is clear to those in the project management team who need it. Team members, suppliers, and vendors should be reminded at the outset of the project of what was bid, your expectations for delivery and cost, and reaffirmation from them *before* they begin the work.

2. *Once under way, keep cost controls in sight and review them on a regular basis.* Once the project has started, ensure that regular reviews of team members responsible for meeting budget requirements are in place.

3. *Don't let your suppliers trade off quality if they have misestimated the project.* One way that suppliers often try to meet budget requirements when they have not been controlling tasks in the project is to cut quality. Without careful observation, this is sometimes not obvious until it is too late. Make sure that the quality guidelines set for the initial plan are being met and that these are not being compromised.

## 6. WHEN TROUBLE COMES KNOCKING—DO SOMETHING

*"Stand up to your obstacles and do something about them. You will find that they haven't half the strength you think they have."*

Dr. Norman Vincent Pearle, *Positive Thinking Every Day: An Inspiration for Each Day of the Year*

Recalling the first time a project or something starts to go bad is a feeling we have all encountered. That knot in the stomach can be a paralyzing feeling, sometimes freezing the project manager into inaction.

### Why

Trouble will come knocking at some time with a project you are involved in, whether you are managing it or just participating, but don't panic. Take a deep breath, consider what the options are and then take action. The greatest leaders are the ones who are willing to take action; standing their ground in the middle of the road like deer in the headlights of an oncoming car just won't change the situation.

FIGURE 9.6 *Surefire Rule #6: When Trouble Comes Knocking–Do Something*

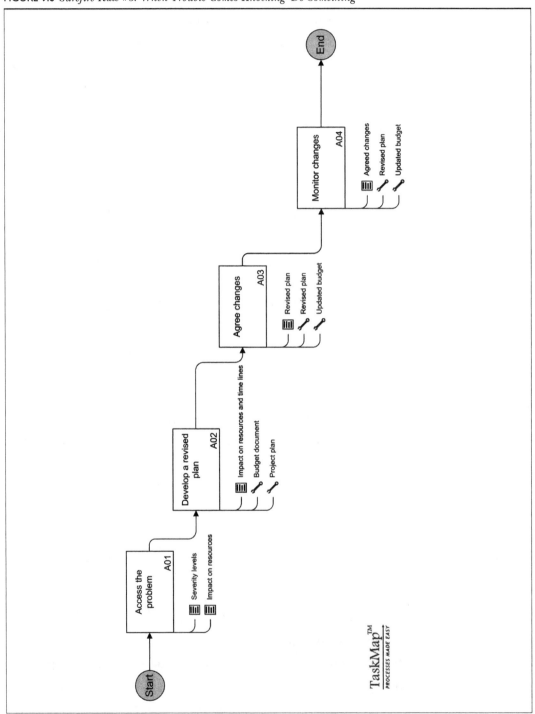

Determine what the problem is and resolve that your first reaction will not be an explosive one. Others in the project are more likely to work with you to fix the problem if they do not feel they are going to be punished and ridiculed for their actions.

## Surefire Practice

1. *Consider the severity of the problem; allow time to consider its impact.* A fire-ready-aim strategy is a certain way to bring the worst from people in a project when it has problems. While you may or may not have been the primary reason for the problem, stand back and consider what the impact is going to be and then develop a rescue plan.

2. *Develop your action plan.* Each project has times when things are going to change; the amount of change is the only variable you have to deal with. Create an action plan that involves the team members' input, the impact on budget, time lines, and other aspects of the project. Submit your change management recommendations and gain approval.

3. *Don't forget to disclose the problem and its impact, and get approval for the action plan.* A final step here, after the action plan has been developed, is to not be scared to bring it to the project owners. After all, it is likely that whatever caused the problem has some impact on their expectations, probably in a negative way. More credit will be given for facing up to the problem, explaining how it occurred and what has been done to deal with it, and then gaining their approval for your recommended actions. Remember, not doing so will have the opposite effect.

4. *Monitor the action plan.* Once the plan and action are approved and in place, monitor the changes to make sure they are successful.

# 7. LEARN NEGOTIATION SKILLS—AND USE THEM EARLY

*"If you come at me with your fists doubled,*
*I think I can promise you that mine will double as*
*fast as yours; but if you come to me and say,*
*'Let us sit down and take counsel together, and,*
*if we differ from one another, understand why is that*
*we differ from one another, just what the points at*
*issue are,' we will presently find that we are not so*
*far apart after all, that the points on which we differ*
*are few and the points at which we agree are many,*
*and that if we only have the patience and the candor*
*and the desire to get together, we will get together."*

Woodrow Wilson

While much of what occurs within a project falls into the management and facilitation category, at some point negotiation skills become very important to your success.

## Why

While facilitation is good, the ability to negotiate with others is a major factor in determining success as a project manager. Nowhere is this more important than at the beginning of the project during the planning phase.

FIGURE 9.7 *Surefire Rule #7: Learn Negotiation Skills–and Use Them Early*

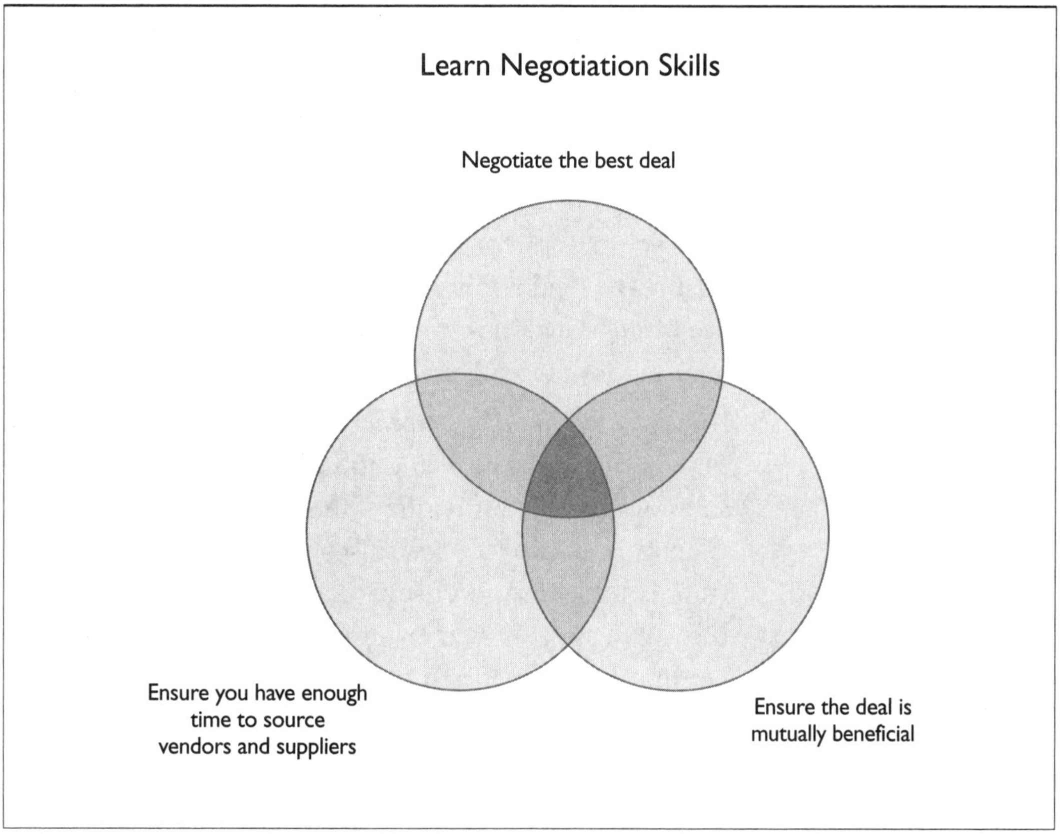

## Learn Negotiation Skills

Negotiate the best deal

Ensure you have enough
time to source
vendors and suppliers

Ensure the deal is
mutually beneficial

## Surefire Practice

1. *Negotiate good terms with your vendors and suppliers right from the beginning.* Effective negotiation of pricing, terms, conditions, and delivery time frames from suppliers is a vital skill in project management. Remember that often the least expensive suppliers may turn out to be the most expensive if they cannot provide the service or product for their part of the project.

2. *Remember the best relationships are mutually beneficial.* Several years ago I worked with a firm that had one of the best negotiators on board, providing you did not want to have an ongoing relationship with anyone he dealt with. This individual was great at buying buildings, equipment, and other inanimate objects. When negotiating with your suppliers, and team members for that matter, ensure the deal is fair for both parties. Pricing and terms are often a deal maker or breaker. Be firm but be fair in your tactics in dealing with others.

3. *Allow enough time to find the right suppliers and partners.* One cardinal sin in negotiation is being in a hurry. If a sales or contract individual can sense you are in a hurry, then do not expect great discounts. Make sure enough time is allocated to ensure that comprehensive quotations can be received from potential suppliers before committing to the final plan.

## 8. COMMUNICATE, COMMUNICATE, COMMUNICATE

There is no such thing as too much communication on a project. Yes, it's time consuming and might not appear to produce immediate results, but trust me this is the big one.

FIGURE 9.8 *Surefire Rule #8–Communicate, Communicate, Communicate*

- Set a schedule
- Determine the best methods
- Have rules in place for times when things change

## Why

Many problems in project management lay at the door of poor communication. For whatever reason, many project managers want to keep this to a minimum. As discussed earlier in the book, in the absence of communication about the status or progress of a project, team members make assumptions. These may not be accurate, and once this occurs, members start taking action based on what they *think* is the status, not what is really going on. For all of these reasons, keeping everyone informed is the first stage of staying in control—if you don't communicate there is no hope of having control, let alone maintaining it.

## Surefire Practice

1. *Set a schedule for yourself.* The first step in good communications practice is to set a schedule for yourself as the project manager. Ensure that you communicate on as regular a basis as is needed for the project, and then start up the process.

2. *Determine the best means to communicate with the team and stick to it.* Early in any project it is important to select the best tools for communication between team members. As many teams are spread around the world today, it is very important to ensure they all have access to the systems you set up.

3. *Put communication rules in place for times when things change on the project schedule.* Because communication is a two-way street, it is very important to put rules in place

for the team. Make sure that you send regular updates
and changes to all the team on a regular basis.

> *"We have come through a strange cycle in*
> *programming, starting with the creation of*
> *programming itself as a human activity.*
> *Executives . . . assume that anyone can write a*
> *program, and only now are programmers*
> *beginning to win their battle for recognition as*
> *true professionals. Not just anyone . . . can do a*
> *fine job of programming. Programmers know this,*
> *but then why is it that they think that anyone*
> *picked off the street can do documentation?*
> *One has only to spend an hour looking at papers*
> *written by graduate students to realize the extent*
> *to which the ability to communicate is not*
> *universally held. And so, when we speak*
> *about computer program documentation,*
> *we are not speaking about the psychology of*
> *computer programming at all–except insofar*
> *as programmers have the illusion that anyone*
> *can do a good job of documentation, provided*
> *he is not smart enough to be a programmer."*

Gerald Weinberg,
"The Psychology of Computer Programming"

# 9. EXPECT AND EMBRACE CHANGE

Change is going to be part of any project; the amount of
change is the variable. Given that is the case, we might as well
embrace it from the beginning.

FIGURE 9.9 *Surefire Rule #9: Expect and Embrace Change*

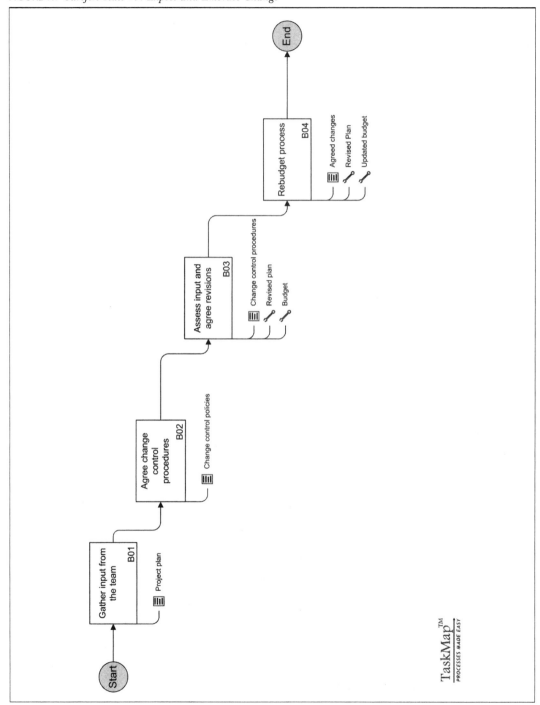

*"Decide what you want, decide what you
are willing to exchange for it. Establish
your priorities and go to work."*

H. L. Hunt

## Why

The project that does not have some change included
from the beginning is extremely unusual. Unless a repetitive
process, like processing a bank check or a help desk activity,
there are usually too many variables in almost any project so
that some change from the initial plan is likely. Managing that
change well is the difference between successful and poor
project managers.

## Surefire Practice

1. *Encourage input from the team regarding changes in the
   project.* Make sure the team knows that communicating
   issues that may affect the schedule or the project team is
   important. Reward an early heads-up that prevents hard
   times later on in the project.

2. *Agree to change control and change management criteria
   early with the project owners.* The project manager should
   not be the only one to understand that change is likely
   and expected in the project. Explain how changes will be
   dealt with in your project with the project owner or
   sponsor. This will start things off on the right foot at the
   outset.

3. *Listen and assess the problem, then take action.* Once a problem is identified, take time to understand its impact. After the impact is known, then develop the action to move the project back on track.

4. *If it is really serious, then rebudget.* When the change is going to be significant, then a new budget may be required. If you think this is necessary, insist on it; otherwise, disaster may follow.

# 10. CHOOSE TEAM MEMBERS AND PARTNERS CAREFULLY

*"I believe that [everyone] is the keeper of a dream—*
*and by tuning into one another's secret hopes,*
*we can become better friends, better partners,*
*better parents, and better lovers."*

Oprah Winfrey

One big factor affecting any project's success or failure is the quality and motivation of those on the team. Choosing your team wisely reduces risks in the project at a stroke.

## Why

The difference between successful completion and utter failure is the team and how it works together. At the onset of any project a unique opportunity is often there, determining who and how you will work together. Picking the wrong members is costly, painful, and frequently leads to all manners of unpleasantness.

FIGURE 9.10 *Surefire Rule #10: Pick Team Members and Partners Carefully*

- *Pick the best for the job*
  - Complement your current team's skills
  - Ensure quality standards and values are the same as yours
- *Check references early and often*
  - Use sources as relevant as possible
  - Allocate enough time to do this well

## Surefire Practice

1. *Pick the best for the job.* Complement subject matter expertise on the project with the best you can find. By careful selection, the best are often not the most expensive, but they usually are not the cheapest. In the long run the overall project costs will be improved by the quality of the team.

2. *Check references early and often.* Ensure that the claims others make are accurate before they are added to your team. Reference checking is an oft missed task during the planning and selection phase—one that is regretted later in the process.

**P**roject management remains that fascinating combination of soft skills and scientific framework mixed with the personalities involved. To many it is a misunderstood enigma; a puzzle that never seems to have the same outcome.

While I have been an observer and practitioner of the art for a long time, I continue to learn on a daily basis. The more I learn, the more there is to refine my own skills and hopefully communicate results to others.

In the vein of providing me with more input to help us all become proficient at this important *sport* feel free to send e-mails with suggestions for future editions of this book to me at:

*mcunningham@harvardcomputing.com*

or write me at:

Michael J. Cunningham
c/o Kaplan Publishing
30 S. Wacker Drive, Ste. 2500
Chicago, IL 60606

I intend to publish any new research and findings on my Web site:

*www.michaeljcunningham.com*

I hope you have enjoyed the read, and hope that your next project is successful, and of course **On Time and On Budget.**

Mike Cunningham
Harvard, Massachusetts
Summer 2006

**brainstorming** Refers to meetings and conferences set up to share ideas in an open and unencumbered way.

**budget** Cost allocated to the project.

**change control** A process set up to manage changes and modifications to an existing project. The project owner and project manager should agree to the change control process in advance.

**controls** Checkpoints to ensure that certain milestones, quality standards, or other guidelines associated with the project have been met.

**cost** The cost associated with items in the project; should be measured against the budget.

**dependencies** Any project element that is dependent on another being completed successfully.

**estimate** Detailed information linking tasks, activities, staff requirements, and resources to their cost structure; the basis for the budgeting process.

**guidelines** Guidance for the successful completion of tasks in the project; can include instructions, business rules, recipes, and general guidelines for the project.

**implementation** The second step of a project that immediately follows the planning phase, beginning with the start-up phase of the project right through the conclusion.

**planning** First step of a project including goals, objectives, and estimates including all the elements in the project.

**priorities** A list of the important goals and objectives to be met by the project.

**process** Tasks and activities linked together in a series of actions that represent a process.

**project management** The act of managing projects using available skills, processes, and systems to achieve desired outcomes from the project in hand.

**quality** Required performance levels and standards needed from the finished project and its components. Quality can also represent standards that have to be adhered to in the project.

**research** Reviewing and collecting of relevant data to assist in the development of the project plan.

**resources** Tools, materials, and systems needed to support activities within the project.

**risk** The hazard level in a project; usually measured on a sliding scale—high to low.

**roles** The job characteristics of individuals participating in a project.

**schedule** A time line with events, milestones, and processes that together make up the overall project schedule.

**scope** A statement reflecting the details of an entire project or part thereof. Typically includes goals, objectives, and milestones for completion.

**stages** Separate phases of a project with their own milestones and schedule.

**steps** Used to describe instructional stages in a project; or specific guidelines for a task.

**tasks** Actions or decisions included in a project; tasks linked together make up a process.

**teamwork** Proactive collaboration and cooperation in a project between team members.

**visualization** Creation of a visual diagram to communicate status and ideas behind the project.

**workshop** Facilitation meeting involving all team members with the goal of creating a defined set of decisions or output; sometimes used in training applications.

# SAMPLE CONTRACT

The following represents a typical subcontracting agreement, courtesy of The Harvard Computing Group. Please see Chapter 5 for a discussion of the characteristics of a good contract.

## SERVICE AGREEMENT

Agreement for consulting services between The Harvard Computing Group, Inc., with its offices located at Devens, MA 01434 (hereinafter referred to as "the Company"), and [xxxx xxxx] located at [xxxx xxxx], (hereinafter referred to as "Consultant"). This Agreement is executed this _____ and shall be effective immediately.

### 1. The Services

The Company may request the Consultant to perform services from time to time for the Company. The services may include requirements definition, consulting, distribution, marketing, market analysis, original research, systems analysis, programming services and/or related activities. If the Consultant agrees to perform the services, the detailed scope of services will be more specifically described in a Work Order signed by each party that will be attached to this Agreement and that shall be referred to collectively herein as the "Work."

## 2. Copyrights and Patents

The Consultant shall promptly disclose to the Company the products of his/her Work hereunder, and those products will be deemed to be a "work made for hire"; and the Company shall be considered to be the person for whom the Work was prepared under the copyright laws of the United States.

The Consultant hereby agrees to transfer, and hereby does transfer, to the Company the entire right, title, and interest to any copyrights and any Work which may not be deemed "work made for hire" under the copyright laws, but which is produced by the Consultant in accordance with the terms of this Agreement. The Company shall have title to any inventions that are made during the course of Work under this agreement, as well as any patents thereon in all countries. The Consultant agrees to execute any documents that may be necessary or appropriate to allow the Company to protect its rights and title in the Work. The Consultant shall not be entitled to any additional payment or compensation for assisting and cooperating with the Company in obtaining these copyrights.

## 3. Independent Contractor

The Consultant is an independent contractor and not an employee of the Company. The Consultant shall not incur any obligation or indebtedness or enter into any agreement, arrangement, or understanding on behalf of the Company.

The Consultant, when performing the Work, shall, at all times, be and remain a subcontractor of the Company, and the Consultant shall look solely to the Company for payment of his/her entire compensation earned in connection with the Work, including expenses.

## 4. Confidential Information

Confidential Information means all of the Company's data, information, algorithms, documents, specifications, designs, methods, and processes, whether disclosed to the

Consultant by the Company or developed by the Consultant in the course of the Work, in whatever form and whether orally or in writing, whether or not marked as "confidential" by the Company (hereinafter "Confidential Information"). The Consultant shall hold all such Confidential Information in trust and confidence for the Company and agrees that he/she will not, during the performance or after the termination of this Agreement, disclose to any person, firm or corporation, or use for his or her own business or otherwise benefit from any Confidential Information.

The above provision shall not apply to information that the Consultant can prove to be in the public domain other than as a result of disclosure by the Consultant, to have been in the possession of the Consultant in writing prior to commencement of the Work or disclosure of such information to the Consultant by the Company, or to have been received by the Consultant other than in connection with the Work from a third party not under obligation of restrictions on use or disclosure of such information.

Upon termination or expiration of this Agreement, the Consultant performing the Work or having Confidential Information in his or her possession shall return to the

Company all Confidential Information of any type including but not limited to drawings, blueprints, descriptions, or other papers or documents that contain any such Confidential Information.

## 5. The Working Arrangements

The Consultants will perform their Work at a mutually agreed location. The Company will provide services and materials to assist with the execution of work on a subcontracted basis. These materials specifically include: business cards, marketing brochures, consulting materials including documentation, flyers, and general materials promoting The Company's services and resources. The Company will also provide certain office services, including telephone message handling and marketing follow-up for Company-sponsored programs. Where material costs are associated with a specific contract, these will be detailed in the Work Order for the contract.

## 6. Consulting Service Fees

The Company will pay the Consultant fees for consulting services on a per-hour or fixed price basis as set forth in each Work Order. Payment schedule will be as agreed with each Work Order. The Company will have the right to withhold payments or portions thereof in the event the Consultant fails to perform services in the manner required by this Agreement.

The Company will reimburse the Consultant for all reasonable travel and other expenses actually incurred in connection with on-the-job services furnished under this Agreement. The obligation, however, is conditional upon such expenses having been specifically approved in advance for the Consultant by the Company. Unless agreed in advance, the Company will not be responsible for any relocation costs or any temporary per diem charges or any related expenses for the Consultant.

The Consultant will submit invoices to the Company as agreed in each Work Order. Each invoice will specifically itemize the fees and expenses for Work assigned the Consultant. Payment terms will be as agreed in the individual Work Order.

The Consultant agrees to maintain necessary and appropriate records so that these amounts can be audited by the Company if the Company so desires, and the Consultant agrees that such records may be audited by the Company upon reasonable notice and during normal working hours.

## 7. Termination

The Company shall have the right to terminate this Agreement with or without cause at any time. Such termination will be effective upon receipt of written notice of termination by the Company. The Company's only obligation to the Consultant in the event of any such termination will be the payment to the Consultant for the services properly rendered up to the time of termination at the rates set forth in the applicable Work Order.

Consultant agrees and understands that any estimates of the amount of time involved in an assignment, which may have been given to the Company in connection with the requested work, shall not be binding upon the Company, and shall in no event be interpreted as any commitment by the Company to continue any assignment for any specific term.

## 8. Liabilities and Warranties

Consultant shall be liable for damages that result from his/her own negligent acts or omissions. The Consultant warrants that all Work and services hereunder will be performed with good professional practices and the state of the art applicable to the Work being performed, that the

Consultant will use his/her best efforts to perform the Work as ordered by the Company and in accordance with the schedule contained in the applicable Work Order, and that the Work shall conform to the specifications set forth in the applicable Work Order. If, during the term of this Agreement and for a period of one year thereafter, the Company discovers that the Work does not conform to such specifications or if program errors are discovered in the Work, the Consultant agrees to use due diligence, at its own expense, to conform the Work to such specifications as was initially agreed and specified within 30 days following written notice of such defects or problems from the Company.

## 9. Indemnification

Consultant assumes full and complete responsibility for all injuries to, or death of, any person, and for damages to property, including property of the Company, arising from his/her acts or omissions, except for damages that may be caused by the Company's sole negligence. The Consultant shall indemnify, defend, and hold the Company harmless from all claims, losses, and expenses including reasonable attorneys' fees or suits for such injuries or damages whether or not such claims are valid.

Consultant shall indemnify, defend, and hold the Company harmless from and against any expense or liability that may result by reason of any infringement or claim of infringement of any U.S. patent, copyright, or trademark based upon the use by the Company of the services, programs, or materials provided by the Consultant hereunder.

## 10. Entire Agreement, Severability, Nonassignment

The provisions hereof, including any Work Orders and other addenda attached hereto, constitute the entire agreement between the parties. This Agreement shall supersede all prior agreements and understandings between the parties and no representations or statements made by any representative of the Company or the Consultant, which are not stated herein, shall be binding. There shall be no modification or amendment hereof unless it is in writing and signed by a duly authorized representative of each party.

A finding by any court of competent jurisdiction that any provision of this agreement or part thereof is unenforceable shall not affect the enforceability of the remaining provisions of this agreement.

Failure of either party to enforce rights under this agreement shall not constitute a waiver of such rights.

The Consultant shall not assign this Agreement or any part thereof without the written consent of the Company. In the event of any such agreed upon assignment, the Consultant shall continue to be liable with respect to all of the obligations or liabilities assumed by it hereunder, and guarantees satisfactory performance of this Agreement by his/her assignee.

## 11. Choice of Law

This Agreement is deemed to be made under and shall be construed according to the laws of the Commonwealth of Massachusetts.

IN WITNESS WHEREOF the parties hereto have caused this Agreement to be duly executed as an agreement under seal as of the day and year first above written.

Signed and accepted on behalf of        Signed and accepted on behalf of
xxxx                                     The Harvard Computing Group, Inc.
..............................................        ..............................................

Name  ...............................................        Name  ...............................................

Title  ...............................................        Title  ...............................................

Date  ...............................................        Date  ...............................................